GRACE *plus* NOTHING

2010 Revised Edition

STUDY
and
GROUP DISCUSSION GUIDE

by JEFF HARKIN

MASTER PRESS

Published by Master Press

PUBLISHER'S PAGE

Grace Plus Nothing Study and Group Discussion Guide/Jeff Harkin
ISBN 978-0-9790296-6-0

MASTER PRESS

Mail to: publishing@masterpressbooks.com

Printed in the United States of America.

Volume Discounts available from Master Press

CONTENTS (Listed by sections)

PREFACE

Briefly, this work is in response to the many requests I've received for a Group Discussion Guide. Though the response to *Grace plus Nothing* has been phenomenal, I thought the Study Guide which I provided in the *Appendix* of the first two editions was inadequate.

I'm using this new Group Discussion Guide myself, with a group at my home church, as a way of testing the material and improving on it wherever I can. But you can help. On the very last page of this Guide I've provided an email address for contacting me with feedback. We are running relatively small printings of this work to facilitate ongoing improvements.

FORMAT

Not pretty but efficient: A format with a neat appearance and a proper outline would have required each new section of this Guide to begin on a fresh page with properly indented subsections, and so on. Instead I've stretched the outline column to column. The effect is to cut the page count considerably which helps control printing costs as well as the costs you'll incur in time and money making copies. I wanted to allow ample space for your notes and simultaneously to save space in terms of page count.

SUGGESTIONS FOR HOW TO USE THIS WORKBOOK:

The author grants permission to make as many copies of this Study and Group Discussion Guide as needed so that each member of your discussion group has one. Beyond recovering copy costs from discussion group members, permission is not given to sell copies.

This Discussion Guide is divided into sections which coordinate with the sectional divisions and chapters in *Grace plus Nothing 2010 Revised Edition*. Your group or your group leader needs to preplan how much material will be practical to cover during each session, usually depending upon how often you meet. One chapter per day from *Grace plus Nothing* is the normal pace. Assignments from this Discussion Guide should be coordinated with whatever chapter assignments you've decided upon from *Grace plus Nothing*.

You will probably discover that there is more material in most sections of this Discussion Guide than you can cover thoroughly in your meetings, so you may need to have the group pick and chose which questions and issues are most important and/or relevant to them. Then just focus on those things and skip whatever you don't have time to cover.

Preparations for upcoming study sessions: Read assigned chapters from *Grace plus Nothing*. And then, before each meeting, read the section(s) of the Study Guide relevant to the chapters you are covering *and* think about the issues raised there. Informed participation and contribution from each group member who feels comfortable doing so is essential for this series to have maximum effectiveness. This material can work for lectures, of course, but it's designed primarily to facilitate discussions.

SESSION #1: INTRODUCTORY DISCUSSION

Before you begin this discussion:

Introduce yourselves to each other, if needed.

READ the "Preface" and "Introduction" in *Grace plus Nothing*.

The **core question** in *Grace plus Nothing* is, "How can I know that I am right with God, now and from now on?" The answer to this question is to completely forsake (repent from) any performance basis for right-standing before God and forever embrace the Grace basis.

The **foundational understanding** undergirding *Grace plus Nothing* rests upon the Bible itself so that your faith does not rely upon mere opinions and experiences. Experiences can be extremely valuable; however, to be trusted as from God, all experience must harmonize with and be in agreement with the Bible. Period! Opinion and/or experience, in and of themselves, prove nothing.

Discussion Questions:

1) Have any of you ever been afraid of cheap grace, sometimes referred to in a derogatory sense as sloppy agape? If so, talk about it, define it if you can. Do you believe that the Grace of God was/is in **any** way cheap? (Later we shall try to clarify and amplify how the Grace of God is free, not cheap.)

2) Reread Romans 6:14. This is a very clear statement that the power of sin is broken only as we come under grace, and Paul makes this statement in the context of some very strong words concerning surrender to the Lord.

  a) Discuss whether or not the opposite may also be true, at least potentially, that to bring people under legalism can effectively bind them under the power of sin. Give this question your best effort now, and we will cover this, and important issues related to this, more thoroughly as we move through this study.

  b) Think about whether or not you believe you have come to the place of needing to relate to the Lord, and thereby develop godly character, on the basis of Grace alone.

3) Is anybody here feeling desperate? Do you think this condition of desperation is positive or negative? Do you have some sliver of hope that the Lord can bring you to where you can say, "Thank God for failure?"

4) Discuss how recognition of our own personal failure to live up to God's holiness is relevant to the Gospel. See, for example, Matthew 5:3 and 6. Can you recognize your need even if you are not desperate? Do you hunger and thirst?

5) Pray for one another or you can ask one person to pray for your entire group before you leave. Pray first for understanding from the Holy Spirit as to how to relate to God on the basis of Grace alone, and, secondly, for genuine hunger for righteousness as God defines this.

For your next Discussion Meeting: Be sure you read Chapters 1-- 6 in *Grace plus Nothing*. Then read and think about the issues raised in this Discussion Guide relevant to those chapters *prior* to your next meeting. Your informed participation and contributions at your group discussion are essential for this series to have maximum (yes, even eternal) effectiveness.

WHY WE FAIL
Chapters 1–6

Before you begin this discussion:

Review and understand WHAT THE BIBLE SAYS. Volunteers read: Romans 3:19–24; 6:23; Galatians 2:21; Ephesians 2:4–6; Romans 11:6, 32–34; Genesis 15:6; Isaiah 53:5, 6, 11.

Discussion Questions:

1) A central issue that needs to be discussed is the fact that the Lord Himself is the authority on righteousness. We may think we are authorities on this subject but our problem is that our sense of true righteousness is tainted/mixed with our knowledge of good and evil. (See Genesis 2:17 and 3:6.) Jesus said that only God is good (Mark 10:18).

What do you think of the assertion that *whoever* God declares righteous **is righteous** (because He is the authority on righteousness), no matter what anyone else thinks about it? Is this good news or does it offend you?

2) Understanding the Gospel: The question is *not*, "Who is *most* righteous *among men?*" Some of us might be okay if that were the case. The issue is God's righteousness! We all fall short of His righteousness and, in and of ourselves, we are powerless to fix the shortfall. Paul explained our powerlessness to fix ourselves in Romans 11:32, using the term "shut up" (NASB), "bound" (NIV), "in the prison of disobedience" (Phillips). In and of ourselves we are dead in our sin. We are literally under the *penalty* and the *power* of sin.

How many in this group have struggled in your own strength to be righteous, trying to earn God's acceptance, approval and blessing? What have you discovered?

a) In the simplest terms possible, the Gospel teaches that, since we have not earned and can not earn God's acceptance, only one option remains: It **must** be a gift. Can you see any other options? **Either we must earn it or He must give it**. Simple and foundational!

b) Is there any middle ground between a gift and something which is not a gift? Either a gift is a gift or it's not a gift. It makes no sense to argue that we must earn a gift.

c) Since, as Jesus said, "It is more blessed to give than to receive" (Acts 20:35), how do you think God Himself gets blessed? Giving: That's His nature and character.

"Bless the Lord, O my soul, and all that is within me, *bless* His holy name" (Psalm 103:1, NASB). Have you ever thought much about what it really means to bless the Lord? If giving blesses God more than anything, what is the #1 thing we can do with our entire being to bless God? Receive His Gift! Believe His Gift!

Thus, Grace is not some miserable, second-class approach to a relationship with the Lord, reserved mainly for compromisers. Rather, His Grace blesses Him as it blesses us. It is His very best.

You want to make Jesus happy? Begin here: The next time you say, "Bless the Lord," pause and add, "I believe You. So I receive unconditional acceptance and right standing before You as gifts. Thank you." Jesus will be blessed, and blessed, and blessed.

3) In *Grace plus Nothing* this question comes up in Chapter 2: "Why would a *good* God turn us over to the power of sin so that we are unable to free ourselves?"

Now that you understand what God is doing, can you rejoice with Paul in Romans 11:32--34 for the wisdom of God in verse 32? Have you ever been angry that the Lord allowed sin to imprison you? Or disappointed with yourself or others before you understood this? Have you begun to see that there is no more effective way for God to demonstrate to us humans that we must surrender to His mercy? Isn't it amazing that such extreme consequences are necessary to induce us to admit that we need mercy?

4) How many Bible passages can your group list which state specifically that salvation, redemption, and reconciliation to God are all gifts? Do you think it might be a good idea to memorize some of these?

5) Do you believe that the Father is truly satisfied with what Jesus did on Calvary? Do you believe that all of your sin, past, present and future, was laid upon Jesus? Does anyone here entertain doubts? Do you trust this group enough to talk about your doubts right here, right now? Jesus died for this. It's safe to admit doubts and to pray for one-another that you will be healed and freed from unbelief. (See James 5:16–18 and I John 1:7–9.)

Doubts about Grace are very common: God's Grace is impossible for the natural man to believe; it is foolishness to the natural man (I Corinthians 2:12–14). The Lord will give you the faith you need. Ask Him.

6) So then, to reiterate from the Bible, we are justified as a gift, and this is according to the righteousness of God, apart from the Law. Right? Who alone has this authority? God has **absolute** authority to declare or to reckon righteous. He does that based on the finished work of the Cross.

7) Absolutes: Remember, absolutes exist in our God. An absolute is something which is always, in all times and places, true. It is never (at any time, in any place) not true. Thus, the next time someone tells you (or you yourself are tempted to think) that there are no absolutes, this is what you need to ask: Are you **absolutely** sure? This assertion, "there are no absolutes," is clearly stating an absolute. Thus: "There are no absolutes" contradicts itself. It is nonsense.

8) In all of your group discussions we want to continue to hone, to sharpen, your capability to share the Gospel with others utilizing Bible truth combined with your own stories. We also want you to continue to develop your understanding related to how to *think about* some of the philosophies you are going to encounter along the way.

9) Pray for one another or you can ask one person to pray for your entire group before you leave. Even though Grace is the only approach to reconciliation to God that makes sense, it seems foolish to the natural man. Understanding and application of the Gospel comes only through the Spirit of God.

MAKING GRACE WORK FOR YOU
Chapters 7–11

Before you begin this discussion:

Review: Can someone define an absolute in one or two sentences?

Review and understand WHAT THE BIBLE SAYS. Volunteers read: Romans 3:24; 5:17; 6:23; 11:6; Ephesians 2:8 and 9; Acts 2:38; I Corinthians 1:18, 30 and 31; Galatians 6:14; Philippians 3:3; Colossians 2:9, 10 and 14; Matthew 18:23–27.

Discussion Questions:

1) We hear many creative definitions of Grace. In *Grace plus Nothing* focus is upon that understanding of Grace which creates and sustains our right standing before God.

a) Many have defined Grace as, "God's Riches At Christ's Expense." Perhaps you've heard this. It's true, but it's vague; it requires further definition. What exactly are God's riches? Without specific definition, this could mean almost anything to anyone.

Given what we've already emphasized in our session on *Why We Fail* concerning the righteousness of God as the central issue in the Gospel, how about this:

"<u>G</u>od's <u>R</u>ighteousness <u>A</u>t <u>C</u>hrist's <u>E</u>xpense!"

Just a suggestion; maybe it works better. What do you think?

b) You may already be familiar with the word *charisma*. In Greek (the original language of the New Testament), *charisma* means gift. Grace in Greek is the word *charis*, which can also mean gift. Each word contributes to our understanding of the other. *Grace, charis,* cannot be understood apart from *gift, charisma,* and visa versa. That's why *Grace plus Nothing* includes so many passages which emphasize that eternal life, forgiveness, righteousness, right standing before God, faith itself, salvation, and the Holy Spirit Himself, are all gifts.

Gospel means *Good News,* and the good news is that, even though none of us has earned right standing before God, He gives it. He has provided all that we need to be right with Him, "in Christ Jesus."

2) Right Standing before God is all about Jesus' finished work at the Cross, not me and my performance. Can you say this? Right now, can you actually experience the freedom this brings? Can you feel the heavy load that this lifts off of you? Perhaps a couple of you can share with this group the effect that this understanding has created in you.

3) Paul points out in I Corinthians 1:30 and 31 how this Gospel eliminates boasting, except that we now boast in the Lord. A simple principle which follows logically from this passage and also, for example, from Galatians 6:14 and Philippians 3:3 is that the actual source of all teaching and doctrine is revealed in whom it glorifies. Does this make sense? Do you need discernment whenever you hear teaching and doctrine? Does this principle give you another tool for doing that? Legalism is never ultimately about Jesus, it's about **you** and how well [or not!] you are performing. This is one of many red flags you will see (one way or the other) in every legalistic system.

4) How and where do you see the power of God? In childbirth? At the seashore? In the night sky? In the scriptures through God's creative power and genius in Genesis? At the parting of the sea with Moses? In Jesus' stilling of the storm, or in His feeding of the 5,000? In raising of the dead? All true, of course. Beyond this, how and where have you expected to see the power of God manifest in your own life and in the lives of loved ones?

a) The Apostle Paul taught that the *word* (Greek, *logos*) or *message* of the Cross **is** the power of God (I Corinthians 1:18). How and why? Obviously Paul was not denying other manifestations and aspects of the power of God, yet he was proclaiming **the** *word of the Cross* **the** power of God. Take *logos*, as Paul used it here, to mean *all that is comprehended in the finished work of the cross*, that is, every aspect of redemption, of forgiveness and reconciliation to God, including Jesus' resurrection. This suggests that all acts and aspects of God's power, no matter where or when, must somehow be comprehended and encompassed in the *word of the Cross*. Can you wrap your mind around this? Not without lots of help from the Lord.

b) Just for review, the consequences of sin are the same in every human being: Apart from Christ, we are under the **penalty** and the **power** of sin. God did this so that He can have mercy on us.

5) Power? Discuss the power of forgiveness (as Jesus defined it). All we ever owed is cancelled and literally gone. In Colossians 2:14, the Apostle Paul defined forgiveness as Jesus did: cancelled debt (NASB Translation). Have you experienced forgiveness this way yet? Freedom from guilt? Freedom from trying to justify yourself? Freedom from trying to explain past failures and sins? Freedom from blaming others? Freedom from feelings of perishing spiritually? Yes? No? To some extent? Can you talk with your group about this?

Note: We are going to cover the remainder of Matthew 18 soon. At that point we will get into the "how to" and the power of forgiving others. We need to do some more work on our Grace foundation first simply because forgiveness of others is feeble and short-lived if driven primarily by legalism and fear.

6) APPLIED GRACE: Could you use some prayer concerning the application of this Grace to your heart and soul? Yes? Please close your meeting asking God to do this in you. Teaching alone can not accomplish this.

NOTES:

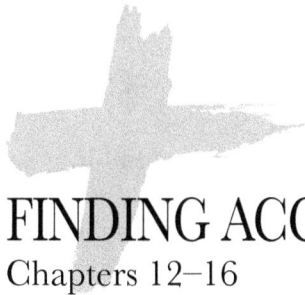

FINDING ACCEPTANCE
Chapters 12–16

Before you begin this discussion:

Review: Someone in the group remind us of the two words which define forgiveness.

Review and understand WHAT THE BIBLE SAYS. Volunteers read: Romans 3:8, 23–26, and 31; 6:14; Luke 18:9–14; Psalm 103:12; 130:4.

Discussion Questions:

1) Let us begin the discussion at the end of this section of *Grace plus Nothing*, the chapter titled "Antinomian Accusations." The Apostle Paul's preaching of Grace generated many vicious false accusations against him as he illustrated in Romans 3:8. I've heard it said many times (and I tend to believe this) that until we are suspected and/or falsely accused of teaching, "Let us do evil that good may come," we aren't really preaching Grace the way it should be preached. Grace scares the socks off of legalists. For one thing they almost automatically jump to the conclusion that we are somehow lawless, against law, when in fact, nothing could be further from the truth. God's Grace has freed many of us from our lawless ways and, although we are still far from perfect, there is now a sweet, ongoing desire for submission and obedience to Him.

Here are two related questions: First, why do so many fight so hard against pure and simple Grace? Second, why does Grace actually scare so many believers? (This probably includes all of us at one time or another.)

a) Is it because it's too good to be true, so maybe it isn't?

b) Or maybe it's because Grace seems so unfair, permitting vast multitudes of undeserving sinners to be forgiven, to walk with God, and to go to heaven.

c) Perhaps it seems that people can sin and get away with it, without consequences. Grace seems very easy to abuse. It seems to let people off the hook much too easily, even freely. Actually, Grace doesn't enable sin nor does it make sin workable, but we will get around to that discussion later. For now, stick with the question of what is so scary about Grace.

d) Consider this: Grace is the one place where we really, finally, lose control. Perhaps Grace is the most, eh, "dangerous" thing about God? It's where He can claim us with no strings attached simply through irresistible, unconditional love and acceptance. Submitting to Grace we relinquish our misguided hope for legalistic leverage, trying to control Him. Now there is only love. Somehow we perceive that this love, this work of the Cross, has the potential to own each one of us; our lives, our souls, our will; without any sort of coercion or manipulation. Truly this is the power of God. His Lordship is His love and His love is His Lordship: John 3:16, II Corinthians 5:14, and Psalm 130:4.

I submit that control issues go a long ways toward explaining fear of Grace plus Nothing.

e) One more possibility: We frequently fear *change*, especially radical change. We may not be satisfied with the way things are, but at least we are in familiar territory. Radical change threatens to move us out of the familiar, out of that which is known, into the unknown. Often, we fear that and fight that. And there are times we resent the change agent; that is, anyone or anything which would encourage us to move.

2) In Chapter 14 of *Grace plus Nothing*, did you understand the distinction between critical thinking and a critical spirit?

Thinking critically is about knowledge, discernment, wisdom, legitimate use of the Bible, and it's also about learning how to think. It's important not only to know *what* to think, but also to know *how* to think about what you see and hear on TV, or on the internet, and even in church. Does that make sense? Critical thinking is instructive, protective, and constructive.

But a *critical spirit* is a judgmental spirit which is very destructive to you and to those around you, even to those you love, and to the cause of Christ. Many of the confrontations Jesus had were with this spirit which, by the way, is frequently a religious spirit.

3) Justification and Sanctification: We will be returning to these two central aspects of the Gospel many times during our discussions. But, first, did you get the basic definitions for each?

a) Sanctification: Set apart for the Lord and for His purposes; dedicated to the Lord. Have you held some other, perhaps more complex, definition of sanctification? Did you see the Lord's heart on this? I hope so. It's one of the main themes of the Bible: God's search for a people He can call His own.

The fact is that in Christ we have been sanctified, set apart for the Lord, *from the very beginning* and our spiritual growth and all manner of obedience and good works are an outgrowth of this sanctification in Christ, having been justified by faith.

b) Perhaps the simplest way to understand justification is *imputed righteousness*, resting totally upon the finished work of the Cross. Imputed righteousness means that God *sees* us as righteous. He *reckons* us righteous in Christ. That's true from the very first breath we draw as believers. I hope that's clear in the book. I know it's clear in the Bible. I suggest you discuss it until you are sure everyone is clear on it.

Here's another analogy which may help: As a justified child of God, you are essentially the same as a new-born baby (in God's eyes). You have no history of sin whatsoever! You can continue in this cleanness every day of your life simply by continuing the same way you began, appropriating Grace. I know that sounds too easy; however, since sinless perfection (authentic works righteousness demands sinless perfection, nothing less) is never honestly a viable option for any human being, is there any other way?

c) Now, think about these crucial questions: Is justification foundational and essential to all sanctification? Or is sanctification necessary in order to *earn* or to maintain justification?

There is much confusion in the Body of Christ when it comes to this. What light does scripture such as Romans 6:14 shed upon this issue? What do you think of the assertion that if we aren't sanctified we can't be justified? This is where your understanding of the Gospel in terms of Acceptance-Based Performance vs. Performance-Based Acceptance becomes relevant. *Big time!* Do God's "rules" for justification ever change?

4) When it comes to the parable of the up-and-outer vs. the down-and-outer, did you see how Jesus asserted His authority to declare someone justified whether or not we agree with Him? This tax gatherer didn't even get his formula for justification right, at least not according to what most of us believe he should have done and said. For example, he didn't promise to quit what he was doing! He was simply in a place of humility (maybe he had lost all hope of fixing himself) and, thus, he asked God to have mercy on him. And Jesus declared him justified (this is imputed righteousness), whether we agree with Him or not.

Get this: IF JESUS SAYS YOU'RE OKAY, YOU'RE OKAY. Period!

SELF-DISCLOSURE and GOD
Chapters 17–27

Before you begin this discussion:

GROUP SHARE: Being careful not to name names, have you ever trusted someone with embarrassing or potentially damaging information about yourself and then later found that they violated trust and told others? What effect does that have on your willingness to become transparent with anybody now? Do you think you can trust God if you become transparent with Him?

Review and understand WHAT THE BIBLE SAYS. Volunteers read: I John 1:7–2:2; Psalm 51:6 and 7; John 3:17–21; Hebrews 9:13 and 14, 16 and 17; Romans 8:1.

Discussion Questions:

1) Begin where we left off last time with this foundational question: IF JESUS SAYS YOU'RE OKAY, WHAT ARE YOU?

Is there any other legitimate authority on righteousness?

2) This section of *Grace plus Nothing* is essentially about how to deal with sin, including how to deal with some of the common tendencies of the sinful nature, and then how to deal with some of sin's immediate consequences. We also include a couple of good examples of how *not* to do it. Bottom line? Nothing works until we do it God's way. This thing is all about Applied Grace.

3) What exactly is sinless perfection? Be aware that sinless perfection isn't simply a matter of our behaviors. Actual sinless perfection must also include perfect thoughts and motives. Jesus demonstrated this in the Sermon on the Mount making the Ten Commandments a matter of the thoughts and heart, not just of behaviors. He also demonstrated it with His life. Sinless perfection *is* required for right standing before God. Legalism can't produce it!

Hopefully, a high percentage of believers want to live as free from sin as possible, on all levels: behaviors, thoughts, and motives. That's a good thing. Certainly we all *need* to get free in as many areas as possible.

But, given that desire, have you ever actually been sidetracked and set back because of inordinate focus on your own performance or on sinless perfection? What was the effect, the final fruit? When you felt you were failing? Or even when you felt you were succeeding?

4) I like what Bob Mumford said many years ago in one of his sermons: "We never realize how far man fell *until* we try to start back." Right! So, if sinless perfection is required, who then can be saved? We know there is only one answer to that question: Jesus died for real sin and real sinners. Thus, according to Romans 3:23 and 24, we **all** qualify for what Jesus did at Calvary. No mere human being could have ever expected (or even dreamed) that our creative, amazing God, through creative, amazing Grace, could turn the awful news of Romans 3:23 into the Good News proclaimed to us in verse 24.

a) Are spiritual fronts helpful in appropriating this Good News? According to Psalm 51:6, what does the Lord require? Why?

Transparency can be really threatening or painful and we have to trust Grace, or most of us won't do it. Have you felt the fear and pain . . . and then the liberation of transparency?

b) How about if we just hide from God (like Adam and Eve did) until we get ourselves fixed up again, until we get spiritual enough to face Him? There are believers who habitually try this. Would anyone here care to share your experience with this approach? What does the Bible say concerning what we need to do with our sin immediately, no matter how many times we've had to repeat the procedure?

c) Grace engenders transparency and therefore facilitates authenticity (and authentic relationships) in every believer who applies it. Why? For one thing, because Grace creates a safe place to get honest. Would you work with the Lord and help create a safe place where believers can get honest with the Lord and with each other?

d) Are you understanding **the way** to a really clear conscience? That's God's will for us. That's one of the main things Jesus died for. Do you understand the concept that, as a result of the work of the Cross, you become in Christ as a newborn baby with literally no sinful past? Have you ever thought of yourself this way before? Now there is no condemnation.

5) Motives: For many years I have contended that if you are truly totally selfish you should immediately turn your will and your life over to the care of Jesus Christ since that is the only way to guarantee your own security and ultimate eternal success.

Whether you agree with that approach or not, we have no record that Jesus ever cast aside any *hurting* person who came to Him, regardless of whether or not that person was behaving selfishly. Does this contradict anything you've previously believed?

a) Ultimately, however, the Lord wants us freed from inferior motives into a realm that only Grace creates. That's why Chapters 24–26 are in the book. I don't want to rewrite those chapters here, so can someone in this group explain briefly how Grace facilitates pure motives?

b) The original sub-title of *Grace plus Nothing* was *Building Godly Character Through Grace Alone*. Are you beginning to see that Grace is the only way that authentic Godly character can ever be built, especially when it comes to motives?

c) In *G + N* Chapter 23, did you understand how all creation shouts the Gospel continually?

6) Suggested prayer need: For more and more safe places in the Body of Christ where people can be transparent, so that Grace may abound, so that authentic Godly character becomes a normal thing in your local fellowship and beyond.

CAN WE FIX OURSELVES?
Chapters 28–34

Before you begin this discussion:

Review and understand WHAT THE BIBLE SAYS. Volunteers read: I Peter 1:13; Romans 7:18–25; 8:1, 2 and 6; II Corinthians 5:17; Colossians 2:9–11; Galatians 3:1--6.

Discussion Questions:

1) Can we fix ourselves? You'll probably say, "Duh! If we could do that we wouldn't even need a Savior." Right, you've got 100% agreement from this author. So, this should be a pretty easy section, and maybe it will be. First, however, some questions:

a) Here is a statement which may sound reasonable to some of you: "Man's problems have been caused by man. Therefore they can be solved by man." You might be amazed how many people actually buy this. What philosophy is this? It's called *Humanism*. It says basically that man is the measure of all things and that man has within himself the solution to all of his problems. Therefore, solving these problems is mainly a matter of enabling mankind to search into its own depths and potential and answers will come.

Question #1: Does it take faith to believe that man, on his own, can solve the plethora of problems which are of his own making? Does human history support such claims?

Question #2 follows from question #1: Which takes more faith? Trusting man to fix it or trusting God?

Question #3 follows from your answers to question #2: Since God won't help with fixing the flesh, since His focus is in the new creation in Christ (see, for example, Colossians 1:27), can you accept that your flesh will never change?

b) Do you agree with the statement that much discouragement in Christians comes from putting some kind of hope in the flesh, in the old man, that it will somehow change?

c) Do you think that this has been the source of some of you own discouragement? If so, perhaps it would be very good idea for you to memorize I Peter 1:13.

2) It might be important for some in your group to spend a few minutes discussing Paul's application of the term *flesh* since, in most cases, he is not referring primarily to the physical body. Is the human *body* synonymous with sin? Review Chapter 29 if need be.

Next question for discussion: Is the human *being* synonymous with sin? I mean, did Paul use the term *flesh* to mean the total *you*? It doesn't seem so. Romans 7:18 indicates that Paul made a distinction between his *flesh* and himself. Psalm 23 says that the Lord restores the soul; He doesn't replace it, supplant it, or obliterate it. Thus, although you were born into this world with a sinful nature because you were born in Adam, *you* are redeemable. Here's a beautiful thing to realize: As a redeemed person, *you* are still *you*! It's just that once *you* were lost and now *you* are found. *You* are simply born twice! Is that a cool plan or what? It is *you* that Jesus wants to save and to keep. Now *you* will become the authentic you, in His design, because you are following the one who knows who you are, because He made you.

3) You are born twice, a new creation in Christ. Do you want to rejoice over the new baby or agonize over the old man?

a) Focus: Perhaps this is the bottom line in this entire section of *Grace plus Nothing*: Where is your focus? What do you spend most of your time looking at and listening to, the new creation in Christ and who you are in Him? Or are you still preoccupied with the flesh?

> *For the mind set on the flesh is death, but the mind set on the spirit is life and peace.*
> Romans 8:6 NASB

I have learned a lot from riding my motorcycle. Okay, okay, laugh at me all you like. But when you are done laughing, I think you will remember this analogy: My motorcycle goes where I'm looking. Yes, it follows my focus. It mysteriously steers itself in the direction of my gaze. (Actually, the same is true of your car, but not usually in such a pronounced way.) I've experimented and practiced with this principle many times and my motorcycle does, in fact, go where I look. This understanding is crucial to skilled, safe riding. Here's why: Say I spot a chunk of debris on the road ahead of me. I sure don't want to hit it or run over it. The natural tendency (and it's very strong) is to keep my eye on that chunk of debris as I try to steer around it. No! That won't work. It's very dangerous and could be deadly. Why? Because my motorcycle wants to go where I look. Thus, to steer around the debris, I make a quick mental note of where it is and then I instantly force myself to focus on the path I want my motorcycle to follow to safely avoid the debris. At that point, even though I'm aware of its location, I'm not going to look back again at the debris. Instead I'll focus on the safest way around it. That's not unlike walking in the Spirit. You never want to maintain focus on the debris. You never want to become sin centered. You'll collide with it! Obviously, you are often aware of your flesh, and you often have to avoid its hazards, however, focus upon it (trying to fix it) is bad news.

It's like when the Apostle Peter was walking on water with Jesus (Matthew 14:28–31). When did he begin to sink? When his focus shifted. Then he became afraid and his faith literally failed. Note: Jesus saved him anyhow. To be sure, that stormy water looked mean and threatening (although perhaps not as mean and threatening as our flesh usually looks) yet, according to Jesus, Peter need not have lost his faith-focus on Jesus.

So, a second time, the question: Where is your focus? Is it on all that Jesus is for you now (I Corinthians 1:30) and therefore all that you are in Him (Colossians 2:9 and 10)? Or is it on the flesh that can't be fixed?

b) Replacement: Discuss this process of replacement when it comes to spiritual growth. You can't be a vacuum, emptied of sin! Rather the Lord pushes out the negative with the positive: beauty for ashes, joy for mourning, forgiveness for guilt and blame and bitterness; faith replaces fear; you'll find many positive what-ifs to replace all of your negative what-ifs, and so on. Do you understand that repentance works, not just in turning from legalism and other sin, but *to* some beautiful things like unconditional love and forgiveness and acceptance and transparency?

Do you think you are still more into avoiding negatives than you are into focus on the positives? Each of you will be different in this, no doubt. Where should *you* begin?

c) Sanctification is always the result, **never** the cause, of our right standing before God. What is the **cause** of our right standing? Always? Can you ever have sanctification without justification? I know we are repeating some fundamentals here. For example, Romans 6:14: Justification by Grace alone is essential to sanctification. This requirement never changes no matter how long you've been a Christian. Thus, sanctification is every bit as much a product of Grace alone as justification.

d) Discuss the sequence of events in Abraham's life which Paul reiterates in Romans 4 and which he advances as God's model for the necessary sequence of events in His redemptive process as He works this in us.

Did Abraham have the 10 Commandments when the Lord reckoned him righteous? Was Abraham circumcised when the Lord reckoned him righteous? Thus, right standing before God can be granted on the basis of faith alone, apart from the Law and apart from circumcision. That's how Paul proved his case for justification by faith without works in Romans 4. Do you think that some Old Testament believers must have been aware that justification could be imputed, reckoned, on the basis of faith alone, resting upon God's promises and mercy? Genesis 15 is very clear concerning this.

e) Do you understand the symbolism of circumcision as it applies to the Lord's redemptive work for us and in us? (G + N Chapter 32) Do you need to discuss this in order to be sure that everyone understands? It is an important concept.

4) Pray: Remember, just because we know this good stuff doesn't mean we can just waltz off and do it, at least not without a lot of help from the Person who invented it! Pray fervently that each of you will walk in this new creation, with your eyes (especially the eyes of your heart) straight ahead on Jesus, the Savior with the nail scars in His hands, ignoring the debris as much as possible. Okay?

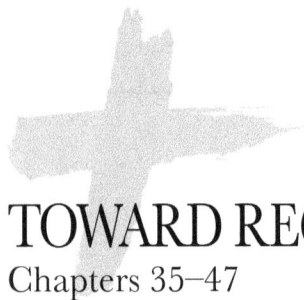

TOWARD RECOVERY
Chapters 35–47

Before you begin this discussion:

This section is an especially long one because it opens up some incredibly important issues. You may need to break it into two group sessions.

GROUP SHARE: Has anyone here had this experience: Have you ever been given a "gift" which had hidden strings attached? Was that truly a gift? How did you feel about it once you came to understand that there were strings attached? Did you proceed to attempt to fulfill the previously hidden expectations of the "giver?" What was your attitude at that point?

Review and understand WHAT THE BIBLE SAYS. Volunteers read: II Timothy 2:25; Acts 5;31; 11:18; John 6:44; Acts 2:38; Philippians 3:13 and 14; Galatians 5:22 and 23 in light of John 15:5, Romans 5:1, Psalm 51:12 and 13 and I John 4:19. Then, on another issue, Romans 8:33 and 34; I Corinthians 15:9 and 10; Genesis 3:12 and 13; and Luke 19:10.

Discussion Questions:

1) You have just read three different passages which clearly speak of God Himself granting repentance. Is this a new concept to you? It is to many believers. Discuss the whole idea that repentance

by God's definition is a gift of Grace, and nothing less. It is this author's contention that, left entirely to ourselves, we don't really know how to repent even if we feel remorse for our sins.

For example, many people are filled with remorse and contrition when they are standing before the judge on a DUI charge. Yet there may be no true repentance there. Sometimes consequences or guilt drive us to be very sorry for something we've done. We may vow never to do it again. In some cases people do keep that vow and also God may use this whole process to bring about repentance. Yet, without the gift of repentance, the process will not lead to redemption or eternal life.

Have you heard preachers say that, unless you are sorry, you haven't repented? Maybe that's true, at least most of the time. The Bible speaks plainly of a broken and contrite heart, and of the poor in spirit, and those terms certainly seem to imply a sorrowful attitude. Yet remorse doesn't necessarily create repentance, at least not by God's definition. The gift of repentance is essential.

(Note: In our section called, "Radical Forgiveness," we will talk about what to do if your problem is that you really aren't sorry for your sin.)

a) Discuss Biblical repentance. What does it mean? Do you need God's help with this?

b) How many times will the Lord allow you to return and repent of the same sin? Have you ever had some voice tell you that if you were truly repentant you would never have done that same sin again? Is this true? If it is, can you then confess *that fact* as sin and be forgiven?

2) We've touched on this before: Discuss the unique blessing of hunger and thirst for righteousness. If you have this, do you understand what a blessing it is? If you don't, are you hungry and thirsty to be made hungry and thirsty? Maybe that's also a blessing. Do you expect to be filled? Or, has the enemy often condemned you in your hunger?

Do you think there is a place of blessing in the Lord where you can be filled and yet simultaneously hungry for more? I think that's the condition we might accurately term "on fire."

3) Paul described the fruit of the Spirit in Galatians 5:22 and 23. We know that fruit trees don't grow just anyplace. Apple trees require one sort of environment whereas orange trees require another. I don't think you will find any banana plantations in Alaska. But you will find more bananas than you can believe in Costa Rica.

a) What is the main point in *Grace plus Nothing* concerning the fruit of the Spirit? Let's answer that question with a couple more questions: Do you think the Lord expects the fruit of the Spirit to grow and thrive *apart from* a healthy environment for growth (any more than a farmer expects to grow bananas in Alaska)? Likewise, can fruit of the Spirit grow in an environment poisoned by legalism? Hardly! Thus, it is going to be crucial to develop understanding and discernment specifically on legalism. We want to be set free if needed. That's one more important thing we must accomplish before this study is finished.

b) The environment required to grow God's fruit is, first of all, the Gospel itself. Did you get this connection in Chapter 42? Do you see how this works, how trusting the finished work of the Cross bears the fruit of the Spirit? Did you catch the fact (in Chapters 38 and 39) that the Holy Spirit Himself is a gift through the finished work of the Cross, that He Himself is our new life in Christ, and that His fruit comes forth through **peace** with God, the **joy** of our salvation and the unconditional **love** we've found in the Father? Clearly, all of this "fruit" is the applied Gospel. (When we speak of transformation that operates only by replacement, applied Gospel is the heart of it.) Locate verses which anchor peace, joy and love in the applied Gospel itself.

c) Have you struggled trying to bear fruit in an environment lacking applied Grace? Have you ever heard the fruit of the Spirit preached in virtual isolation from the Gospel, almost as if it's a separate issue from the work of the Cross? As if spiritual maturity is somehow a step or two *beyond* the Gospel? Almost as if those who are spiritually mature should not need Grace anymore?

Can this work? The Bible says grow *in* Grace (II Peter 3:18), it never says grow *out* of it! Grace is your God-given environment for growth and fruit bearing.

d) Beyond your own personal walk in Grace, what can you do to help make your local fellowship and Church a healthy environment for growth? How about repentance from gossip, judging, cliques, complaining, unrealistic expectations of ministers, and letting 20% of the members do 100% of the work? How about praying for your Pastors? How about tithing? This is not a bunch of legalism (because we need not apply it legalistically), it's just stuff that helps make a healthy church, and a healthy you.

What if you think the Lord is leading you to change churches? Sometimes He does that. How about making the transition in the most healthy possible way: for one thing, not defending your decision to leave with a bunch of criticism. You know what I mean? What you probably need to say is that you believe the Lord is leading you to a different fellowship. I'd go tell the Pastor directly if at all possible, and not just drop out of sight.

4) Would you agree that true worship is also a function of a healthy environment for growth? Do you see the sad enigma of work for the Lord that does not flow from supply? It's like pushing your car vs. putting gas in the tank.

It may not be so easy to sort out what to do if you've had your cart before your horse, serving from an empty tank, so to speak. You may be serving in some capacity where you can find a replacement. Then again, you may be doing something where you see no immediate replacement(s) and it would be totally irresponsible to just drop what you are doing and walk away. And there is a third possibility: Sometimes, unless you move out of the way, the person the Lord wants to replace you with won't emerge or come forward. No two situations are exactly alike. Can you share this dilemma with your group and ask prayer for wisdom or for replacements, or whatever? Somebody in your group may have some helpful input for you and you may need to meet later and discuss that.

5) Stretching you understanding of an environment for growth *way* out there. I have attempted to show you from my own life how the Gospel created an environment for growth, even in the absence of any perceptible faith. Quoting from *Grace plus Nothing*, Chapter 43:

> *The grace of God is radical, more radical than any love you have ever imagined. Believe it. Or, just pretend, as I did – just act as if it's true.*
> *If you will act on God's grace, it will work; I don't care whether you initially "believe" it or not.*

All I can say is that just pretending like God's Grace could apply to me changed my life. Sounds ridiculous and unorthodox I know. But you read my story. It is amazing Grace; truly Grace plus Nothing! I've challenged several people over the years to do this. I'm presently communicating with a person who has seen his faith literally created out of nothing (because he didn't believe in God to begin with) by simply trusting, or *acting as if*, this Good News applies to him. Now, in his own words, he's "on the road home." He's a full-on believer.

Three questions: First, has there ever been a season in your life when pretending that Romans 8:28 and 29 applied to you would have been a wonderful light at the end of the tunnel (if you had known that you could do this)? Second, do you know anyone who really, really needs to know about this radical option right now? Third, can you think of a way to give it to them?

6) What does the common practice of defending ourselves have to do with all of the above? This section of *Grace plus Nothing* is called, "Toward Recovery," and the first step in any recovery process, especially in the application of the Gospel, begins when we stop blaming others, defending ourselves, and we simply begin to own (own up to) our feelings, issues, sins, mistakes, shortcomings, etc. Actually, we never ever get to true repentance and forgiveness until this wall of self-defense either collapses of its own weight, the Lord takes it down, or we voluntarily begin to take it down.

Defending ourselves is basically self-justification, so it contradicts God's clearly stated purpose to be our justifier. (Review Romans 3:26.) Do you think self-justification, or the lack thereof, is a pretty good litmus test of how we are abiding in Grace? Do you discern that *all* legalism amounts to self-justification?

When is self-defending necessary? See *G + N* Chapter 44.

Do you think this is ever necessary before God?

Are you getting in the habit of forgetting your excuses and immediately running **to** Him when you sin?

7) Pray for the gift of repentance. Pray for hunger to be made hungry, if you need that. Ask the Lord for wisdom to discern legalism. Ask Him to grant that you will be able to create an environment for growth in yourself, then in your family, then in your church, and so on. Ask the Lord to empower you to actually trust the Gospel. Ask the Lord to remind you to maintain your focus where it belongs. Pray for service that flows from supply. Speak out some personal needs and pray for and minister to one another.

BREAKING OUT OF LEGALISM
Chapters 48–55

Before you begin this discussion:

GROUP SHARE: Ask group members to talk about the circumstances and situations in which they have really enjoyed competition. Conversely, when have they *not* enjoyed, and maybe even hated, competition?

Review and understand WHAT THE BIBLE SAYS. Volunteers read: I Corinthians 1:27 –31; Romans 9:30–10:4; 8:1; Isaiah 14:12–15; Psalm 110:3; II Corinthians 4:7; John 12:31–33.

Discussion Questions:

1) This section shouldn't be difficult to understand simply because most of us have been immersed in Performance-Based Acceptance all of our lives. It's the definition of the world system. Many of us have enjoyed some aspects of PBA very much, yet we have all also, at times, hated it. Our enjoyment of the system generally depends on our ability to compete and to win in one arena or another, and there are many arenas.

In this section of *Grace plus Nothing* we want to focus not only upon "in your face" varieties of PBA, but also upon forms of legalism which tend to be more subtle. For example, most forms of "Christian" legalism appear to encourage spiritual growth. Also, adherents to various legalisms may be extremely sincere and zealous, like those zealous legalists Paul described in Romans 10:2. Nevertheless, every form of legalism undermines applied Grace because all, without exception, pervert or distort the Gospel, one way or another. Be reminded that, "even Satan disguises himself as an angel of light." (II Corinthians 11:14 NASB) Discernment is crucial.

Right up front let's emphasize this one salient point: If you want to understand the Grace of God in Jesus, one good way to do it is to take the world system (PBA) and reverse it, turn it on its head. What you will have then is ABP, Acceptance-Based Performance: That's the fruit of the Spirit, and *all* that the Lord wants, flowing freely and powerfully out of His unconditional acceptance through the work of the Cross. Have you got that? Good, then the rest of this study will be easy.

2) One great example of ABP in the midst of the world's PBA system is the unconditional love you will find in many families. Have you seen this and/or actually experienced it yourself in any relationship anywhere in this world?

3) Okay, *G + N* Chapter 53, "No Shotgun Wedding." I hope you got the point here; I hope I didn't offend you. It is a graphic analogy which is intended to expose widespread legalistic *abuse* of Jesus' Bride (the Church).

This Chapter requires our attention early in this discussion of legalism simply because it pretty well says it all! The way this term "shotgun wedding" is being understood and applied here is, of course, different from how we've understood it in our culture: The shotgun wedding has been commonly understood to mean a wedding *forced* upon a couple because the young lady gets pregnant. But the way we are using and understanding this expression here has to do with Jesus' Bride being somehow forced and coerced to the altar.

Our first question is: Why should someone so magnificent and so full of love and truth as Jesus need His Bride to be forced to His side? Can you picture the marriage supper of the Lamb as a shotgun wedding? Do you agree that, if this were the case, Jesus would be the laughing stock of all creation, especially among all of those principalities and powers who derided Him here on earth?

Second question: How do you think Jesus feels concerning the *abuse* of His Bride? Does He take it lightly? Or does He hate it? Does He want that stopped?

Why use the term abuse? What does this mean? How do we typically recognize abuse? I've gotten an accurate description of abuse from friends of mine who are counselors. They say that virtually all abuse, whether political, domestic, or spiritual, has three major components: **Manipulation, intimidation** and **invalidation**. No doubt you know first hand what manipulation is, and what intimidation is. How about invalidation? In this application, invalidation means that what you think and feel doesn't matter. The only validity is with the abuser: What he, she, or they think and feel is what carries weight. You will be taught or told what to think. You will seldom be taught how to think!

Hard core legalism is usually all of the above. It is spiritual abuse, manifest in countless forms and incantations. Under abusive spiritual leaders you will no doubt be told (or it will be implied) that, if you leave their group or church (or get yourself thrown out), you won't be right with God. As a general rule, abuse is about *control*.

a) Have you encountered abuse? Have you seen it? Even in Christianity?

b) Are you aware that, since we are in a free country, you need not take such abuse?

c) Not all legalism is quite so hard core. Milder forms are far more subtle. But can you see that, on some level, all legalism is abusive? Do you understand that legalism is sin?

d) Think about this: Do legalists attempt to use any of these three abusive tactics against the Lord Himself? Do you think legalism amounts to abusing the Lord?

e) Can you see how manipulation, dead religiosity, and similar variations of abuse usually signal the *absence* of the power of God? Psalm 110:3 is pivotal.

f) What's the difference between persuasive preaching and manipulation? You will find a lot of persuasive messages, teaching, preaching, testimonies, and stories in the Bible.

g) Please remember, Grace opposes *legalism* not *law*. Grace does **not** militate against the disciplined life or the life which is guided primarily by purpose and mission. Life without purpose and discipline is usually chaotic and practically without meaning. It often ends tragically. God's Grace creates discipline as well as a deep sense of purpose and mission.

4) "Conviction vs. Condemnation:" Here is another important key in discerning whether you are living in legalism or Grace. Romans 8:1 is an excellent place to begin.

Discuss the difference between the conviction of the Holy Spirit and condemnation, as well as the impact of each upon you personally: One is pushing you away from Him and the other is drawing you to Him. How do you deal with each of them? Apply the finished work of the Cross when the Lord is convicting you and apply the finished work of the Cross when the enemy is condemning you. Either way, you receive forgiveness, cleansing, and repentance if needed.

Is preaching that "convicts" the Church legitimate?

5) *G + N* Chapter 54, "Clay Pots:"

a) First, even Pastors and preachers who have no intent to abuse may inadvertently do or say legalistic things from time to time. They may make some rather stupid mistakes if you hang around them long enough. They may also have some pretty big gaps in their armor. Even though, as James says, such leaders/teachers are to be held to a higher standard, where does the clay pot fit into God's design? Paul freely admits that his clay pot shows. Right?

b) Is it potentially dangerous for a leader/teacher to somehow hide the clay pot? Why?

c) Why must you embrace your clay pot, especially if you want to be mightily used of God?

d) How would you define a clay pot? As human-ness? As having limitations? As the walking wounded? As having residual emotional damage and/or other residual faults and shortcomings? Anything else you can think of?

e) Does spiritual maturity eliminate the clay pot?

f) Have you ever judged your Pastors, spiritual leaders, your Mom or your Dad, your husband or your wife, your boss, etc, for what turns out to be the clay pot which they can neither shed nor cover up?

g) How hard have you been on yourself for being a clay pot?

6) Becoming Like The Most High? (*G + N* Chapter 49)

     a) Discuss the satanic nature/origins of this sin as it is revealed, for example, in Genesis 3:5 and Isaiah 14:12--15. Do you see how rejection of God's righteousness and of His finished work links back directly to the tree of the knowledge of good and evil?

     b) Discuss how normal and common it is for sincere believers in their zeal for the Lord and in their ignorance of God's righteousness, to get drawn onto this evil merry-go-round. Take as your primary text Paul's observation and burden concerning Israel from Romans 9:30–10:4. Where does true repentance and submission enter the picture?

     c) What is the primary deception in the so called New Age Movement? Do you know of any religion or faith, outside of faith in Jesus, that actually provides Grace plus nothing to its believers/followers as the basis of right standing with their god(s)?

     d) Discuss faith(s) or religious systems that deny the existence of sin. Are these systems examples of God's Grace? Why not?
Our God does not deny sin nor does He minimize sin, nor does He compromise His holiness in any way in order to accept us. How is it possible that He remains absolutely just, yet He forgives and justifies sinners?

     e) It is not legitimate to use, "to obey is better than sacrifice," (I Samuel 15:22) to rebuke applied Grace. Make sure you understand why this application of I Sam. 15:22 is lousy exegesis and why, therefore, it cannot be used against sincere but imperfect Christians who need to appropriate daily forgiveness and cleansing according to I John 1:9–2:2.

7) Discuss "lifting Jesus up" (*G + N* Chapter 55) in terms of its generic usage in the Body of Christ as compared to how Jesus Himself applied it very specifically in John 12:32. Caution, you don't need to reject the generic usage, just understand what Jesus was saying.

     a) Do you think Jesus was giving us an obvious and essential key to advancing His kingdom?

     b) Is all "church growth" synonymous with advancing the Kingdom of God? Why not?

     c) Is the Gospel still relevant in this modern day and age?

     d) Is moralizing completely wrong or is there a way to serve as a prophetic voice for righteousness within our society without coming across as mere critics of sinners behaving as sinners? Some preachers have accomplished this simply by always explaining the Gospel within any messages they give on morality/immorality. Let's pray right now for our preachers.

APPROACHING THE LAW WITH GRACE
Chapters 56–58

Before you begin this discussion:

GROUP SHARE: Have any of you traveled or otherwise spent time in any country or culture where there was no clear rule of law; where most authorities did whatever they felt like at the time, whatever was right in their own eyes, and they were in some cases persuaded by bribes? Did you feel safe there? When you returned home, did you feel grateful for the rule of law we enjoy here, even though it is far from perfect?

Review and understand WHAT THE BIBLE SAYS. Volunteers read: James 2:10; Colossians 2:13 and 14; Romans 7:7; 3:20 and 31; Galatians 3:24; Exodus 20:1–17.

Leviticus 16:1–31 Note: This is supplemental reading. You'll probably want to cover this outside of group.

Discussion Questions:

1) When does God's Law become our friend? Does it ever really become our friend?

2) Is there any benefit in meditating on (maybe even memorizing) the Ten Commandments? Is the author a legalist because he recommends this?

3) What do you think should be done to a doctor who has diagnosed some terminal condition for a patient in plenty of time to intervene and treat and cure, but who never informs the patient of the diagnosis or cure? Have you come to where you thank God for doing the responsible and loving thing in giving you His diagnosis and cure?

4) Why can't the Father always explain why?

5) Do you understand the distinction made in *Grace plus Nothing* between the numerous sacrificial and ceremonial aspects of the Law and the moral laws themselves? Do you think mankind would have been healthier had we paid more attention to things God said in the Law concerning hygiene and sanitation?

6) Do you understand how to use the Law *lawfully* (I Timothy 1:8)? Without creating legalism?

7) The reference in Leviticus is included because, if you will study it, you will see how the Law foreshadows what Jesus did for us at the Cross. You'll find much in the Law which is a type or a foreshadow of redemption, of the heavenly Tabernacle, of the Lord's eternal dwellings, etc. The writer of Hebrews points out many very important and interesting aspects of the Law in this regard. Check it out. You'll love it!

JESUS plus NOTHING
Chapters 59–70

Before you begin this discussion:

GROUP SHARE: Ask two or three in your group to talk about how they learned to balance and ride a bicycle. Did they get this balance from hearing instructions from an adult? From reading a book on it? Or from trial and error? Did they have training wheels? Did someone run alongside, holding them upright until they got it? Can anyone in the group explain balance graphically enough to enable a beginner to balance a bicycle without someone running alongside to help?

Know and understand WHAT THE BIBLE SAYS. Volunteers read: John 14:6; Jeremiah 23:6; I Corinthians 1:30; Colossians 2:9 and 10; II Corinthians 1:20; Isaiah 7:14; John 1:1–18; 17:23; Romans 5:8.

Discussion Questions:

1) Learning to live our lives **in** Christ is in many ways analogous to learning to ride a bicycle. We can read about it, we can hear about it from our friends, we can watch somebody else do it, but it's only as we live **in** Christ ourselves that we finally actually get it. The Lord has sent someone to us who *runs along side*. He is, of course, the Holy Spirit, the Comforter, Greek, *parakletos*, comforter or advocate, also understood as one who comes along side to help. Just as the gift of balance usually comes rather suddenly, that is, you suddenly realize you're balancing, and a big smile breaks across your face, so it is with this Grace life in Him.

2) Another simple, yet graphic analogy: How many of you are struggling to get into this room right now? Why not?

What do you have to do to abide in this room?

3) Discuss how the "in" takes the "if" out of all of the promises of God. (*G + N* Chapters 59 – 61)

a) How often are you confronted with the "if" concerning who you are *now* in Christ?

b) It's definitely legitimate to have to demonstrate our faith as we live day to day. In fact, the initial *demonstration* of our new confidence that the "if" is gone in Christ is probably going to be that we cease all our striving to earn right standing before God because we have peace with God (Galatians 5:22 and Romans 5:1).

Stating this same thing another way: Faith has legs. We know that true faith in Christ will definitely change our behavior. True faith will be demonstrated. Think about James' requirement that we show our faith in our actions (James 2:17-20). Let me suggest that, for some of us, this requirement is initially met when we finally rest from our own works and enter into God's rest (Hebrews 4:9 –11); when our consciences are "cleansed from dead works to serve the living God" (Hebrews 9:14). What do you think? Is rest a valid demonstration of faith in Christ?

c) Take some time and see how many "in" verses you can find which describe where you stand, sit, belong, or abide, etc., in the Lord. Read these passages out loud, or perhaps even better, let members of your group call out passages as they locate them, write them down, and review them in the next few days as needed.

d) If you wake up tomorrow morning and you don't feel "in," where are you? In or out? Who/what is your authority to believe this?

e) How did you get to be in Adam? And in Christ?

4) Is your Savior totally adequate? Can you rest in that knowledge?

a) Jesus can *not* be some new species. Why does this matter? Have you come to the realization that Jesus is neither less than God nor more than man; that He is fully God and fully man?

b) Perhaps you need to talk about why we can't discount the virgin birth. How does it define the Incarnation, "God with us"?

5) Living in the righteousness of Christ: Imputed and imparted! I Corinthians 1:30 is relevant over and over again in this study, together with Jeremiah 23:6.

a) Faith in faith: Jesus frequently validated someone's faith affirming that *their* faith was why He healed them or set them free or, more importantly, how they recognized Who He is.

Utilizing the following questions, spend some time discussing faith and how well it works for just about anybody, Christian or not:

~Do you have faith in faith? Under what conditions?

~Do you think that everyone exercises faith in one way or another, whether they be Christians or not? Do you have to be a follower of Jesus to exercise faith and/or positive thinking?

~Even though the objects of faith may vary widely, does faith work even in the so called secular realm? For example, in sales? In athletics? In recovery groups? Between parents and children? In developing new products and technology? Even in isolation from faith in God?

~Does it make sense to have faith in faith?

~Describe why or when faith *without* God *can't* work.

b) Faith in Jesus' faith: If we build our walk with God in all that Jesus is for us, that is, in His righteousness, there is stability. For example, Jesus' faith is unwavering, always strong; He is the Author and Finisher of faith, and He is right there in you and with you right now, and He is your righteousness. Your own personal faith probably ebbs and flows, some days strong and some days not so strong. Can you have faith in Jesus' faith or does that seem ridiculous?

c) Do you think that sometimes we take ourselves too seriously while we don't take Jesus seriously enough? Can you laugh at your clay pot sometimes and just trust Jesus?
Do you focus too much on your own faith instead of resting, walking and ministering in the faith of Jesus?

Do you think that Jesus was always serious while He was here? Do you think He was always fretting about His disciples' shortcomings? Do you think He had some laughs with His disciples and others? Do you think Jesus ever had fun doing His ministry with people?

d) Do you think, if you lighten up and trust Jesus' faith and His presence with you, in spite of (and maybe even because of) your clay pot and all of your shortcomings, that you become dangerous to the devil?
As you learn to live this new way, do you think that you might rise up and overcome in situations where others are likely to go down in discouragement?

e) Has your awareness of your own shortcomings or weak faith ever kept you from sharing Christ with someone (when you actually had the opportunity), or perhaps from praying with a friend who was sick?

Here's a *positive* what-if to throw against all the *negative* what-if's that get thrown at you in this arena: *What if,* from now on, you do those things just because you know that Jesus is your righteousness, that He will be all you need for the ministry at hand, and that He will be right there with you, being all that He is for you?

Do you think, if you take Him more seriously and yourself less seriously, that this Christian life might be easier? Do you think you might be more fruitful? Do you think you might actually have more fun than you've ever had in times past, serving the Lord?

f) One well known adage says, "Make it hard on the Lord and easy on yourself." Does that offend you or do you think there is some truth to it? His yoke is easy and His burden is light (see Matthew 11:30).

6) Now that we understand living "in Christ," need we say much concerning the old formula which is so frequently chanted in such empty and unthinking ways, "In Jesus' Name?"

Does the use of Jesus' Name as a mere formula force God to do whatever we ask because of His promise in John 14:14? Is that how Jesus meant "in?" Or did He intend for us to actually *be* in Him, as we are now? The name Jesus expresses who He is. Do you now think that praying in Jesus' Name probably means the same thing as proceeding in Christ and all that He is for us?

How will this effect your prayer life and the results you see?

7) And, if you seem to see no results? What will you conclude concerning the love of God toward you?

8) What is the grounds for our boldness in prayer?

9) Pray for one-another.

CONFIDENT LIVING
Chapters 71–73

Before you begin this discussion:

GROUP SHARE: How has confidence (including self-confidence) or lack thereof impacted your ability to succeed in life? Do you believe that confidence is generally crucial to success?

Review and understand WHAT THE BIBLE SAYS. Volunteers read: I John 5:13; Micah 7:8–10; Hebrews 12:5–13; 13:5; Romans 8:38 and 39; Psalm 2:1–5.

Discussion Questions:

1) This section, "Confident Living," flows quite logically from all we've just taught and discussed concerning our lives in Christ. Now we move much more deeply into the effects of Grace, the fruit of Grace, if you will. This goes beyond self-confidence and positive mental attitude, as valuable as those qualities can be.
Obviously Grace bids us trust in Christ for our redemption, not in ourselves. But do you think Grace militates against any and all self-confidence? Do you think there is a healthy sort of self-confidence which is devoid of arrogance, which does not contradict our trust in Christ, and may very well be a direct result of our trust in Him?

2) "The Security of the Believer" and "Confident Living:" How confident can you be in the Lord if you believe that your ongoing security in your relationship with Him (and also your hope for eternal life) rests upon you? I submit that such an error could and would undermine our ultimate trust in Christ. Here's why:

a) This particular error, which I'm going to refer to as the *lose your eternal life* error, amounts to a nullification of Grace!

Addressing this error directly: If you think you can lose your eternal life, then, obviously, *it's up to you* to *keep it*. Are you that arrogant? Are you really willing to put that much confidence in your own goodness, knowledge and fortitude? Okay, you believe you have Scripture to support your position. Yet, no matter how you rationalize this error as faith in Christ, you actually believe that your salvation (and therefore, your eternal life) rests upon you because you believe that *you* can lose it. That's the only conclusion we can draw. You need to think hard and long about the following question because your *belief* may be leading you to a shocking and fearful conclusion. Here's the question:

So, you believe you can lose your eternal life. If this is your *belief* then this is your *faith*! What do you want us to say, "According to your faith be it unto you?"

This horrifying ramification must be accepted by any *lose your eternal lifer*. This author has been around a lot of *lose your eternal lifers* and one of my observations is that these folks usually apply their threats of loss of salvation to somebody else. They will argue vehemently that eternal life can be lost. So then, they must admit that this is their faith and they must face the apparent consequences to themselves and to their loved ones, not just to somebody else.

If you are a *lose your eternal lifer*, do you really want to live under this guillotine? **You should be overjoyed to hear that you are in error and you cannot lose your eternal life.**

b) This *lose your eternal life* error/threat has been another shotgun held to the Bride's head. Do you see that? Does it not throw the Bride into performance-based acceptance?

c) Do you see how the term "Security of the Believer" rather than the term "Eternal Security" helps eliminate confusion? Both terms indicate that believers cannot lose their salvation, yet the "Security of the Believer" seems most clear concerning who has this security. Either term works, of course.

d) Eternal life is eternal, and the Lord wants us to know that we are presently living it. That's why I John 5:13 puts knowing that we have eternal life in the present tense. Therefore, since the Lord doesn't contradict Himself, *we* must be misunderstanding or misinterpreting any Scripture that seems to contradict this. Hebrews 6 is a good example: Please read Hebrews 6:1–9. First, any careful reading of Hebrews reveals that it was written to believers, specifically to Jewish believers who were under persecution and, therefore, they were considering returning to temple worship and sacrifice in order to escape persecution.

Second, Hebrews 6:1–3 cannot be teaching that we should grow out of Grace or beyond Grace simply because Peter says that we are to grow in Grace (II Peter 3:18).

Third, I submit that any *farmer* who reads Hebrews 6:1–8 will conclude that it does *not* teach that we can lose our eternal life. Why? Because many farmers have burned their ground. They all know that the ground itself never burns. The weeds burn. The ground may get scorched but it is never consumed by the flames. Study this passage for yourself. In this analogy **the "ground" (NASB; "land," NIV; "earth," KJV) itself is analogous to the believer,** so that, if/when that ground gets burned, it makes sense that the weeds are burned but the ground remains; it is not lost. Likewise, the believer who gets burned is not lost. He/she will no doubt be scorched and in pain from the consequences of sin *and* the Lord's discipline. The weeds, however, are gone! I Corinthians 3:12–15 sheds additional light on this understanding of Hebrews 6.

Next, and this is totally relevant to the understanding I've just presented to you: Listen carefully to the writer of Hebrews as he concludes his stern exhortation. He clearly *affirms* that he believes the best for these Christians, *things that accompany salvation*, even though he is speaking to them in such stern tones (see vs. 9). Obviously, he does not believe that they are going to lose their salvation, yet they could face some severe and painful consequences if they return to a legalistic system of justification which, "can never, by the same sacrifices which they offer year by year, make perfect those who draw near" (Hebrews 10:1 NASB).

Contemporary legalisms don't resort to animal sacrifice but they certainly resort to systems of self-justification which can never make perfect those who draw near. Thus, the warning to the Hebrew Christians in Hebrews 6 is applicable **today** to any Christians who return to and/or who cling to legalism. That's what the Hebrew Christians were thinking of doing. Thus, ironically, if you interpret Hebrews 6:4–8 as a *lose your eternal life* teaching, you have put yourself exactly where the writer of Hebrews warned his readers not to go!

e) God's Word doesn't contradict itself: Following verses 4–8, could the writer of Hebrews immediately and blatantly contradict himself? Please read through to the end of Chapter 6. You will see that the writer goes on to teach very clearly that our confidence and the hope which anchors our souls rests securely in God's own promise and oath: Our anchor is secured, "by two unchangeable things in which it is impossible for God to lie . . ." Our anchor (our hope and our confidence) is sure and steadfast, not because we must somehow keep ourselves, but because of the unchangeableness of God's promise and oath.

Context! Context! Context! It is essential to read this entire letter if we want to understand this author's intentions in chapters six and ten (passages which are frequently misunderstood and misinterpreted). For example, Hebrews 12:5 – 13 makes it very clear that our author is speaking of discipline rather than eternal damnation for God's own children.

f) "Those who were once enlightened, and have tasted of the heavenly gift, and of the good word of God, and of the powers of the age to come, and have been made partakers of the Holy Spirit" (Hebrews 6:4). This is how the writer of Hebrews describes the believers he is addressing. I have seen people exactly like that fall away, haven't you? Let me ask you this: Did you write them off? Or have you continued to pray for them? Frequently they have given up on themselves as well as on Christianity and God!

Do you think God has given up on them? True, they often suffer some terrible consequences. They get burned off! There is one very strong weed that gets burned off for sure, if it's there: Legalism!

It may be impossible for us to renew the scorched earth again to repentance but don't write these people off. Here's why: "With men this is impossible, but with God all things are possible." (Matthew 19:26 KJV) In context, Jesus was speaking concerning the impossibility of any rich person being saved, and, in response to questions which arose concerning this, Jesus addressed the impossibility of *anyone* being saved. His answer? It is humanly impossible, but God can do it!

I submit that the writer of Hebrews was not questioning God's ability to save *anybody*, even in the worst case scenario, no matter how far beyond the reach of Grace they may seem to have fallen.

g) Has anybody here seen or experienced this painful, costly process in action? Was legalism part of the cause for falling away? Such people can wind up being among the Lord's best eternal examples of His mercy. Many have moving stories of His faithfulness.

3) Whew! I sure hope this discussion helps you move beyond the doubts and fears, the challenges to your faith, and the challenges to the Gospel, that get planted through teachings such as the *lose your eternal life* error. Hopefully the discussion wasn't too tedious. I hope I didn't step on anyone's toes, but if I did, I can't apologize. Distortion or invalidation of the Gospel must be confronted in no uncertain terms.

Now, we are going to change the subject. That fact, in and of itself, may bring a smile to your face! We are about to lay hold of several powerful weapons of our warfare. Here's one:

3) You want a powerful weapon?
    One that's totally fun to use?
      That's scientifically proven to be great therapy?
        Something that God says He also uses?
          That powerfully expresses confidence in Him?
            That constitutes one of the greatest confessions of faith there is?
            That audibly expresses joy?
              That audibly expresses thankfulness?
              That audibly shouts VICTORY?
  Laugh! That's right, I said laugh. Laugh out loud!
    Laugh at whatever scares you.
      Laugh at whatever makes you nervous.
        Laugh at your enemies.
          Let that river flow from your innermost being.

Great belly laughs! That's what God has. Psalm 2:1–5 says that's what God does: He laughs at His enemies. Nothing scares God. Nothing threatens Him. (And you are in Him.) Add to that the fact that Satan, in all his pride, is utterly humiliated when he is derided with laughter.

a) If you could hear the sound of heaven right now, one thing you would hear is lots of laughter. This is not just the Lord laughing at His enemies, it's the Lord enjoying His children.

In Romans 8:31 (KJV) Paul says, , "If God *be* for us, who *can be* against us?" That's a rhetorical question which insists upon this answer: Nobody!

b) Studies of laughter therapy have shown that laughter contributes to the healing process in seriously ill patients. Do you think laughter has the potential to generate healing for wounded emotions and perhaps even for deep hidden areas of the spirit?

If you are having a bad day, can it help pull you out of a funk?

c) Think again about demonstrating our faith with our works. What will you think if I suggest that one such demonstration of our faith can be laughing more and worrying less? It makes sense. Laughing out loud at adversity or condemnation can be your powerful expression of faith that God is in charge, that He is the one with the authority to declare righteous, that you are okay because He says so, and that all things will work together for good! That's all true. Right? You need as many tools/weapons as you can get to bring your emotions into line with the truth. Laughter in faith has explosive power against enemies such as worry and fear.

d) There may be someone in this group to whom this question is relevant: Are you tired of expecting the worst and getting it? Think about it. Does this description at least approximate the approach to life, to problems, or to people, which you often *feel*? Expecting the worst? This is probably such a habitual feeling that it seems like reality. No doubt it's worked its way into your head! Would you like to blast that lie?

e) If you think of laughter as an expression of faith and joy and gratitude then it becomes a powerful spiritual weapon capable of pulling down strongholds, of bringing every thought into captivity to the obedience of Christ. If you don't believe this, I challenge you to do it sometime amidst trying circumstances. James says to count it all joy when you encounter manifold trials. (See James 1:2 and 3.) Laughter is one way to express that.

f) You probably realize that there are many times when you can decide to laugh, by choice, at will; not in every circumstance, of course, and not in every place, but almost! I know there may be members of this group who are too self-conscious to do this, but there may also be a couple of folks among you who can. So, if you are gathered someplace where you can make noise, try this right now: Start laughing. Do it volitionally, with focus on who Jesus is for you. And, if there is something you are worried about right now, laugh at that!

I hope you had the audacity to do that. If you did you probably found it is contagious, and your more self-conscious members probably joined the fun.

4) HERE IS YOUR ASSIGNMENT FOR THE WEEK: In addition to the readings you'll be doing for your next session, practice laughing: When you are stuck in traffic, when you do something dumb, even when other people see you do something dumb. Especially laugh at accusations and disqualifications thrown at you by the devil: These are fiery darts. Laughter is part of your shield of faith. It can quench those darts. Do it, you'll see!

RADICAL FORGIVENESS
Chapters 74–78

Before you begin this discussion:

Review and understand WHAT THE BIBLE SAYS. Volunteers read: Isaiah 40:1 and 2; 53:5 and 6; Matthew 18:21–35; Romans 12:19; James 5:16.

**Speaking of ultimate weapons (as we did in the preceding section), forgiveness is the ultimate, ultimate, ultimate weapon. It may well be the most important weapon in God's arsenal, I don't know. But I'll bet it's up there in the top two or three!

Discussion Questions:

1) No matter what your sin or your problem is, you can always be reconciled to God. Grace in fact does go as far as the curse is found. He has paid double for all our sin. Did you understand the concept of pushing the work of the Cross as far as you have to in order to walk in forgiveness and reconciliation? Beginning with your sin itself all the way through to the issue of not being sorry for it (if that's a problem), bring it all to the Cross. Is there any other way to fix your lack of remorse (if that's a problem) than the cleansing promised in I John 1:9?

2) This section on "Radical Forgiveness" deals primarily with personal issues we may have with unforgiveness and the consequences we often suffer when we harbor unforgiveness (even toward ourselves). Remember the saying which is common in the recovery movement (original source of this quote unknown): "Unforgiveness is poison we swallow thinking that someone else should suffer."

That's exactly how it works: Unforgiveness opens us up to all sorts of torment as Jesus said it would in Matthew 18: 34 and 35. (Note: This Scripture is about consequences of unforgiveness here and now. There is no mention of hell in these verses.) God intends this consequential torment for our good: He's letting us know that something has gone terribly wrong, in us. We've swallowed deadly poison! Now the torment motivates us to discover this and to deal with it.

3) Why are some people afraid to forgive? I have talked with many who feel that, if they forgive, they are letting down their guard and thereby opening themselves to ongoing abuse. We certainly are not recommending that anyone go back into abusive or otherwise dangerous situations. So, let's try to clear that up first. Here is something I put together for our recovery groups concerning forgiveness and boundaries which I've distilled primarily from Cloud and Townsend's vital book on boundaries: [1]

---

[1] Please see Note on the last page of this Study Guide.

Boundaries: Don't forget, forgiveness doesn't mean that you must make yourself vulnerable to continued abuse, abusive language, or hurtful or negative behavior, or to a toxic relationship, or to inappropriate requests for money, etc. On the contrary, forgiveness will help you set healthy boundaries because forgiveness itself is a boundary which protects your mind and heart from bitterness and resentment, and from obsessive thoughts about retaliation. Thus, forgiveness will make you stronger and more assertive and more sure of yourself in potentially threatening or negative situations. It will help you deal directly and boldly with abuse or inappropriate behavior. It will help you free yourself from toxic relationships. Remember, the Lord forgives all day long and He still maintains clear and healthy boundaries, which means no one can invade and take control of Him even though He continues in the tender vulnerability of His love!

Forgiveness will help you feel much more secure in your relationship with the Lord simply because, in the act of forgiving, you will also experience His forgiveness (which is already there for you) more deeply than ever before in your life. So, you will be a more secure person, more bold and assertive, expecting the best. Yes, in general, you will just feel much better!

Note: Your personal *boundaries* differ from your personal *walls* in that walls (as protective as they may seem) actually block communication and make healthy relationships difficult or impossible. Boundaries, on the other hand, are essentially lines in the dirt which indicate where another person must stop and where you begin. They provide visible, audible evidence concerning who you are (if you express them clearly and boldly to others, as needed). For example, your boundaries indicate how you will allow others to speak to you, or touch you. But you must let others know where you draw the line. Unlike walls, lines in the dirt will not block your communication; they enable it.

Forgiveness will help you stop others from violating your personal boundaries because you can respond much more objectively, being relatively free from bitterness and hostility and retaliatory behavior. You want to fix the situation and help yourself heal and grow at the same time. Is that correct?

Therefore, forgive! That's what Jesus recommends.

PLEASE TAKE THE TIME TO TALK AND TO PRAY WITH ANYONE IN YOUR GROUP WHO FACES THIS SORT OF SITUATION, WHO WANTS TO FORGIVE, BUT WHO MAY NOT KNOW AS YET HOW TO PROCEED WITH HEALTHY BOUNDARIES

4) If the statement concerning forgiveness and boundaries makes sense to you, then we can move on to other barriers to forgiveness. Here's a main one: "If I don't *feel* forgiveness then I can't forgive, right?" How does that line up with Jesus' and Paul's definition of forgiveness? Thankfully, it doesn't!

a) The forgiveness confession in *Grace plus Nothing* expresses forgiveness as a *choice*, a choice to cancel debt, whether we feel like it or not. Have you begun to exercise this freedom yet? It may not seem to you like this will work but take it from someone who, many years ago, had more hate and unforgiveness than most of you can imagine. Well, some of you can because you have similar torments. But this works. If you'll do it consistently for a while, you'll see. What have you got to lose?

b) Keep in mind that many of the people we need to forgive don't deserve it. The word forgive is interesting in that it consists of the words *give* and *for*, almost like *give before*! Yes, that's what it amounts to: We *give before* anyone deserves it, exactly as the Lord has done for us.

c) If you are a victim of serious physical, sexual, verbal or emotional abuse, you may need to go through this forgiveness confession many times toward your abuser. But, if you don't forgive, then you will continue to be tormented by the abuser, even if he/she/they are long gone.

People who abused you aren't here to change or to apologize to you, or to repent. **You are here**, so the only person you can work with is you, to be released from the torments of unforgiveness: from obsessive thoughts, reliving horrible experience(s) from the past; from obsessive thoughts of revenge; or, for some of you, from terrible false guilt as if you yourself somehow caused or encouraged the abuse.

5) Another barrier to forgiveness: Living under the manipulative control of another person and/or living as a co-dependent can produce a lot of resentment in you and, ultimately, unforgiveness. Living under abuse (as we've defined it earlier in this series) does this. Now that you know better, if you passively submit to an abusive system (including a spiritually abusive environment), if you fail to deal with it effectively, it militates against the fruit of the Spirit.

Caring too much what other people think usually has the same effect, and this is typically more *our* issue than it is *theirs*. See that? By caring too much what they think we put ourselves under their control, even if they don't desire to control us.

6) Does the need to make amends or to make restitution contradict Grace? Not unless somebody makes it grounds for right standing before God. What if you've stolen something or done some serious damage somewhere? That stuff may still be hanging over your head and the Lord wants you as free as you can possibly be from your past. Restitution may be part of that.

You may need to go to someone and just ask them to forgive you, whether you think they will or not.

One very important qualification: If you do make amends or restitution, will it do more harm than good? Sometimes somebody can be seriously hurt by you trying to make amends. Unloading your conscience at somebody else's expense is a very bad idea! It may be best just to allow the work of the Cross plus nothing to deal with your bad conscience and save the other person much unnecessary heartache. Sometimes, however, coming clean with everybody is not optional simply because there are legal issues which must be faced in order to put the past in the past. Ask yourself, what would true love do here? Ask your group, if your group is a safe place in terms of confidentiality. Do you have a confidentiality agreement and understanding in your group? If so, share your heart and get some prayer. Ask for wisdom so that you'll know what the Lord would have you do about amends and restitution.

7) What continues to be the most difficult barrier to forgiveness for many of us? Forgiving ourselves. There are so many ways that this problem manifests itself, from sabotage of our own success or relationships, to beating up on ourselves in various awful ways, to deadly habits, all the way to suicide.

Somebody said to me once that there isn't a single Bible verse that says to forgive ourselves. Okay, are there Scriptures that, though they never mention this specifically, actually apply?

If we say we believe that the Lord forgives us, yet we refuse to forgive ourselves, what does that say concerning our faith? "I know the Lord forgives me but I won't forgive myself!" Can we walk in the Spirit in this attitude?

Have you put your faith into action in this vital area? There is no better time to begin than now! What exactly do you hate and/or not forgive in yourself? Name all of it specifically, using the forgiveness confession on yourself, right up to and including the phrases concerning cancellation of your own debt and owing yourself nothing. (There's seldom a need to use the last couple of phrases of the confession regarding apologies or admissions of wrong since they seldom apply when applying this confession to ourselves.) You are going to feel and do much better as you learn to walk in forgiveness toward yourself.

8) Finally, this level of forgiveness requires the Holy Spirit. Let's not forget that the Lord hasn't left us to do hard things like this on our own. Bring your unforgiveness to the Cross and give it up! Remember that repentance is a gift. Ask God for repentance from every sort of resentment and unforgiveness, then give it up, quit the beatings, quit obsessing over the one(s) you've resented. Remember that vengeance belongs to the Lord, so give it back to Him. Revenge is His problem now, not yours. Period!

NOTES:

CORRECTION WITHOUT REJECTION
Chapters 79–86

Before you begin this discussion:

GROUP SHARE: Ask any members of your group to share a bit about how (or if) they were disciplined in their homes, and looking back, how they feel now about the rules they had to follow, the chores they were expected to perform, etc. Discuss things like, did they have to eat dinner at the table with the rest of the family? Did they have a curfew? Did they have to pay for their own car and insurance? Were they expected to perform academically? Were any of these things perceived by them as conditional acceptance, or simply as disciplines? If they were not being subjected to conditional acceptance, looking back, do they now appreciate the disciplines and expectations? Has this made them better people, husbands, wives, citizens? Maybe more able to handle the real world?

If they had none of the above, looking back, do they feel cheated? Has lack of discipline in youth made it more difficult for them to do life as an adult? Maybe so, maybe not; perhaps they got discipline elsewhere, in sports or in the military. Perhaps someone among you can address this issue from such a background.

Finally, discuss consequences at home for violating the rules. Were these consequences dealt out in anger or in a matter of fact sort of way? Were they dealt out fairly and even-handedly? Whatever the situation was, did you somehow benefit from suffering consequences?

Review and understand WHAT THE BIBLE SAYS. Volunteers read: Genesis 2:16 and 17; Hebrews 12:4–13; Titus 2:11–13; Matthew 6:3 and 4.

Discussion Questions:

1) Do you understand how suffering, in and of itself, does not produce spiritual maturity? What does produce spiritual maturity by God's definition? Have you experienced how the Lord can make any bad thing work for you?

Your cross to bear is not defined primarily in terms of suffering. Agree? Disagree?

2) I know you are glad that the Lord's correction is not rejection. In Hebrews 12:4–13, could you see where God's correction is guaranteed for us believers because we **are** accepted, we are in?

I'll never forget when, during one of my lukewarm, more or less uncommitted seasons, God said to me (inside, not in an audible voice) concerning His call and mission: "You can go the easy way or the hard way, Jeff, but you're going!" See, He's not messing around, He's not playing church, He is our God and Father. Period! That understanding has been a great comfort to me. He is in this with us for the long haul. Has God's willingness to discipline become a comfort to you?

3) Consequences, boundaries, limits: One of the gross misunderstandings of Grace that's out there among believers is the misconception that, if we teach the free gift and the unconditional acceptance of God's Grace, we are saying that we can all do as we please and get away with it.

That's the real reason some Pastors and teachers are afraid to teach both justification and sanctification through Grace alone, even though that *is* the Gospel.

Are you clear that unconditional acceptance doesn't validate evil behaviors or attitudes? Do you understand that Grace doesn't make sin work? That Jesus didn't die to justify sin?

Genesis 2:16 and 17 make it clear from the beginning that God, in His mercy, placed a very clear and inflexible limit on mankind. How and why is this limit a blessing?

Does God take sin lightly?

There are also some consequences of sin that, in Christ, we will never experience. What consequence(s) did Jesus take in our place?

a) Violation of design: It's usually our own wickedness that corrects us without any immediate action on God's part. Even under Grace we are not without limits, are we?

Design dictates use. We can like it or lump it. There is an understanding of righteousness which fits very well here: right-use-ness. That's insightful, isn't it?

b) Discuss Paul's experience wanting to fix himself, which he describes freely and graphically in Romans 7. What were the consequences of the "I," "I," "I" approach, attempting to get free from the power of sin?

4) How can our salvation be in no way synergistic (in Ch. 83, review what this means) and yet we end up being the Lord's co-workers, His partners, working hand in hand with Him?

When "giving alms," have you come to the place Jesus spoke of where it's such a part of you that you are no longer keeping score? If you haven't arrived there yet, don't feel condemned and, whatever you do, don't give up! It's about growing in Grace, that's all. Did you experiment copying your own signature? Which approach looks authentic? Does it make sense that authentic Christianity is ultimately this normal?

5) Why is James' letter incorporated into this particular section of *Grace plus Nothing*? For one thing, James wrote a strongly corrective letter. Can we receive it as correction without rejection?

a) We've discussed James' assertion that we live (i.e., that our lives reflect) what we actually believe. Would you say that this assertion applies to all human beings no matter what exactly they believe?

Taking into account the patience of God bringing us believers to the place where Grace becomes a way of life for us, is James correct?

Given what we know of Grace, it is important to think about this: Do all believers (especially, new believers or believers who are just coming to understand applied Grace) evidence their faith in the same way? And, is all evidence of true faith externally observable? We need to be careful here. This is where legalism can easily kick in! Some churches look for one kind of evidence and other churches look for another. The recovery movement often looks for things that churches may miss in their lists of evidence(s) of the faith.

Internally, what can we expect as our first-fruits of trusting Jesus? Romans 5:1.

b) James does mention the law (1:25) and he seems to view it pretty much the same as we've suggested in *Grace plus Nothing*. Now look at some of the subjects James covers (evidences of true faith in Christ) and judge for yourselves whether or not these things are Grace in action:

Here are just a few samples. I hope you have time for this. If not, maybe set aside some time to do this at home. You will be blessed! Volunteers read: James 1:2 and 3, the joy of facing trials. Vs. 5 – 8, wisdom through faith and the instability of doubting God. Vs. 17, God is good and also transparent (no shadows). Vs. 19 and 20, this passage is prominent in the Anger Management recovery program I lead. Vs. 27, much better to think of religion this way. Ch. 2:1 – 4, partiality. Vs. 13, mercy triumphs over judgment. Vs. 14 and 19: It seems clear that James was using the term "faith without works" in an entirely different way than Paul used it. Here's what James meant by faith without works: It's "faith" like the demons have who "believe" in God to the point of terror, yet their belief involves no "works," that is, no turning to Jesus in repentance or trust. So you see that what James meant by faith alone is "belief" like the demons have (vs. 17), and, thus, James' "faith without works" is certainly not the same as what Paul meant: Paul's use of faith without works (Romans 3:28) clearly does NOT refer to belief like the demons have, but it very clearly means trusting Christ. Therefore, do you think Paul would have agreed with what James said concerning faith? Ch. 3:1 – 12, would to God that the Body of Christ would seriously heed this passage. Vs. 16 and 17, jealousy and selfish ambition and the wisdom of God. Ch. 4:7, authority over the devil. Vs. 13 – 15, arrogant presumption. Ch. 5:7 and 8, faith and patience. Vs. 14 – 18, faith and healing, faith and transparency, faith works even in our own human frailty. Vs. 19 and 20, the wonderful fruit of sharing Christ with other sinners!

This letter from James is beautiful, a work of art that reflects the grace life. But you'll need to be firmly planted in Grace before you can read the whole thing and see the beauty.

REDEEMING YOUR EMOTIONS
Chapters 87–89

Before you begin this discussion:

Review and understand WHAT THE BIBLE SAYS. Volunteers read: Psalm 42:5; John14:1; II Corinthians 10:5.

Discussion Questions:

1) This is a very short section, yet obviously extremely important, for many reasons. Did everyone understand that even though we *feel* emotion there is a definite, important distinction between feelings and emotions? What is the difference?

Why do we need to feel? What are the positives and negatives of feeling? When is pain our friend? How about pleasure?

2) Self-talk generally occurs inside our heads, yet sometimes we also verbalize it.

a) Discuss your self-talk. Is it usually more positive or negative?

b) How does that effect your day? Your relationships? Your ability to succeed?

c) How many old tapes run in your head on a more or less regular basis?

d) Do you see what a valuable tool/weapon Psalm 42:5 can become in your life?

3) Preach the Gospel to yourself. Perhaps you've heard this before.

a) Many folks constantly listen to Christian CD's and TV, etc. in order to keep themselves built up and on track. Have you tended to think of this approach as the only means available to you to effectively build yourself up in the faith? I'm not trying to discourage regular church attendance or regular ingestion of recorded teaching and song. These are wonderful provisions which the Lord uses regularly in this author's life. Yet, let's ask, have you been too dependent upon external voices? What about your own knowledge of Scripture and of the Gospel? Can you preach it to yourself? Maybe you need to memorize more grace passages. You can use positive self-talk all day long *and* it will also help you sleep at night.

b) In using this tool/weapon, you often need to verbalize the truth to yourself **out loud**. You'll find that your words spoken to yourself have power. Okay, if someone hears you doing this they may conclude you're crazy. But, believe this: It's so powerful it's usually worth the risk.

4) Trusting Christ more than we trust our feelings and emotions:

a) Just like self-talk, do your emotions or feelings ever lie to you?

b) Have you recognized how feelings are often perceived as truth and reality by many folks in our culture? Have you yourself ever lived as a hedonist? That is, "If it feels good, do it, and if it feels bad, avoid it."

c) Do you need to feel God in order to believe He's with you? How stable is that?

d) Can you build a marriage or a career or a future using your feelings as your foundation, or as your primary ongoing motivation? What else does it take to be successful in any of these endeavors?

e) Having said all of that, do you think it's a good idea to stay in touch with how you are feeling, even though feelings may be untrustworthy as your primary authority? Do you have a tendency to deny your feelings and/or emotions? Do you think that, quite often, your feelings might be telling you the truth?

Feelings can be very important in letting us know when something is wrong, or when something is right. Let's not forget that! Given that our feelings often require objective confirmation, there will be times and places where you need to trust, and not ignore, what you feel. This can actually be discernment from the Lord. Remember, feelings are terrible masters, but they are also wonderful servants.

Is there anyone here who has ignored your feelings when you should have paid attention? Conversely, have you had situations where you trusted what you felt and now you are glad you did?

f) Is it hard for you to get in touch with how you are feeling? Or is it difficult for you to talk about it?

g) Fact, faith, feeling: That's probably the simplest way to explain the chain of authority as we see it in the Bible when it comes to applying the Gospel. Does this make sense? Are you willing to be patient with yourself and with others in this process of retraining your self-talk, thoughts, feelings and emotions to make them captive to the obedience of Christ?

5) Can you talk about painful emotions (such as a grief process) that you have gone through in the past? Were there any ultimate benefits? Was there any ultimate healing? Was there any ultimate resolution of conflicts with others? It may be beneficial to others in your group to speak (briefly as possible) of your own experience with painful emotions and feelings which turned out to be beneficial in the long run.

STUMBLING BLOCKS TO GRACE LIVING
Chapters 90–92

Before you begin this discussion:

GROUP SHARE: Talk about the influence of people who, for one reason or another, were significant in your life: Specifically, what impact did these people have in shaping your attitudes and behaviors before you came to Christ? And, same question, how about now, since you've turned your life over to Jesus?

Review and understand WHAT THE BIBLE SAYS. Volunteers read: I Corinthians 15:33; Psalm 23:1; Matthew 6:24 and 33; II Timothy 3:1 – 5; I Timothy 6:6 – 11; III John 2.

Discussion Questions:

1) Who are the major influences in your life?

a) Do you need to find more positive friends? More Grace people? Have you given yourself an environment for growth?

b) If you are married to an unbeliever who isn't encouraging you in your faith, what does the Bible say about that? I Corinthians 7:12–16: This situation can be a very positive thing for both of you and for your children.

On the other hand, if you are seriously considering marriage to an unbeliever, possibly even hoping to change that person later, that isn't fair to you or to the other person. What does the Bible say about that? II Corinthians 6:14 no doubt applies here. Walking away from that relationship may hurt terribly right now, yet you may well be walking away from much greater hurt later on.

2) Covetousness, greed, money.

a) A lustful or covetous person can never be satisfied. Do you agree with this?

b) The Bible seems to have no problem with money or riches in and of themselves. The problem is when money owns us rather than the other way around. Would you agree with this assessment?

c) A lot of debt results from covetousness, would you agree? Is debt a stumbling block in your relationship with God? With your spouse? With yourself? Do you enjoy being in debt?

What sort of debt could be justifiable or even necessary, under favorable circumstances, at least in the short haul?

Nevertheless, sooner or later, preferably sooner, would you like to live debt free?

There are some excellent Christian teachers out there who specialize in money management according to Kingdom principles. Get in on that. Don't let debt enslave you.

d) Is there more security in counting your money or in making your money count?

3) Of course, we can make a much longer list. What do you think needs to be added to this short list of stumbling blocks to Grace living?

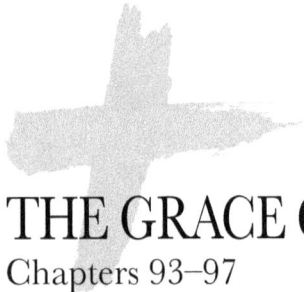

THE GRACE COMMISSION
Chapters 93–97

Before you begin this discussion:

Review and understand WHAT THE BIBLE SAYS. Volunteers read: II Corinthians 5:14–21; Proverbs 27:5 and 6; James 5:19 and 20; Acts 1:4 and 8; John 3:34 and 35; Matthew 28:18--20; Colossians 1:13 and 14; I Corinthians 1:26-29.

Discussion Questions:

1) Would you be able to explain the condition of mankind and the way of salvation to a friend who is open to listening? Can you do this from the Scriptures? Why is it important to be able to explain the Gospel using the Bible? It can be as easy as memorizing John 3:16 and 17, Romans 3:23 and 24 and 11:32, I John 1:9, Ephesians 2:8 and 9, Revelation 3:20 and John 1:12.; maybe a couple more. Or, make your own list of the scriptures which God used to bring you into relationship with Him; these will, no doubt, be easier to memorize.

List Your Scriptures Here:

Also, in sharing your faith, do you have the confidence to weave in some of your own story?

a) Do you know what needs to be included in a very simple "sinner's prayer?" Could you pray this with someone in case they don't know what to pray?

b) Practice: Years ago, when I was in sales, we had sales meetings nearly every morning, primarily for practice. We would often role play. We would practice answering questions, countering objections, presenting features of our products, reviewing common mistakes, etc.

I firmly believe that a lot of believers seldom share the Gospel simply because they never have practice doing it. Would you be willing, as a group, to practice with each other? Maybe do this during this meeting or, better yet, make a plan to do it soon.

2) Discuss the need for death and eternal hell. Hell exists because God is good. Can you actually conceive of death and hell as a promise rather than a threat?

3) Are there any of God's Marines in this group? That's good! This Grace is for you as much as any of the rest of us. Aren't you glad? Have you come to feel at one with us common soldiers?

4) If you are a common soldier, have you generally disqualified yourself from any significant role (other than giving money, which is important and we don't want to minimize this ministry) in fulfilling the Great Commission?

a) Are you aware that Satan wants to disqualify every believer in one way or another?

b) Most of us have thought of ourselves as disqualified at times. Why exactly are you disqualified? Age? Divorce? Too far from perfect? Lack of education or training? Maybe you know you are not a preacher or a missionary and you see no other avenue to participate? Perhaps you are not in a position to go to a mission field because of responsibilities for family, etc?
Are there more approaches to participation in the Great Commission than as a preacher or missionary? List two or three of these:

c) Have you ever considered getting more equipping, either through more formal education or through disciplined self-education, or maybe working with a group (on the job training) toward this end?

d) Tithes and offerings count. No need to talk about this as a group unless the Lord leads. Between you and the Lord and your spouse, if you are married, have you been listening to the Lord concerning significant investments to advance the Kingdom?

e) Somebody here may need to memorize:

We the willing, led by the unqualified, have been doing the unbelievable
so long with so little that we now attempt the impossible with nothing at all!

Are you aware that such folks as these, with the Lord's blessing and anointing, are capable of sweeping advancement in and for the Kingdom of God?

5) Pray: We've covered a lot of important ground here today. Remember your missionaries.

**And don't forget, it will be profitable for everyone in your group to practice sharing this powerful Gospel. It will help you put aside fear and self-consciousness. It will help you grow in confidence. You are where you are loved, so mistakes will be significant only as learning experiences. Right?

SEEING HIM CHANGES YOU
Chapters 98–107

Before you begin this discussion:

Review and understand WHAT THE BIBLE SAYS. Volunteers read: II Corinthians 3:6, 16–18; Isaiah 6:1–8; Hebrews 1:3; Psalm 139:6–18; Mark 10:18; Colossians 1:15--17.

This section is Theology 101! It's also Christology and Soteriology (study of the Cross and the work of the Cross). We've already observed that our lives will ultimately reflect what we really believe. Now, let's go one step further: Our lives will ultimately reflect what we really believe about God. That's why, "Seeing Him Changes You." Therefore, the crucial question is, "What is your concept of God?"

Discussion Questions:

1) I submit that, if we want to know God, it is best to begin with Jesus. Why? Because He told Philip, "He who has seen Me has seen the Father" (John 14:9 NASB). Thus, let's begin at the very end of this section, the very last reading, "Scars."

a) Check John 20:27. Has it ever struck you as odd that Jesus has a resurrected, glorified body, yet He still bears His scars from the crucifixion?

b) Has it occurred to you that you'll never know God intimately apart from Jesus' scars, that is, apart from the work of the Cross?

c) It may not be appealing to think in terms of seeing and touching scars, yet do you think this may be important in relationships which you care about?

Do you think you may have judged some folks superficially, not knowing their scars?

Do you realize that you may know some people who are worthy of much respect (they may not *look* like it) simply because of how far they have had to come just to get to where they are today?

d) Scars, as we see them here, are not about morbid self-pity or getting sympathy.

e) Maybe we all *get to* keep our significant scars (essentially healed wounds). What do you think of that? Do you even want to keep yours? Maybe, in the Kingdom of God, scars are beautiful.

2) Whatever drives you, whatever motivates you, will reveal your concept of God:

a) "Avoiding Failure vs. Seeking Success:" I'm hoping to accomplish at least three major objectives through this analysis of motivation:

One is to get more perspective on what makes legalism (PBA) tick: Avoiding Failure. Which of the kids in the studies mentioned in *Grace plus Nothing* succeeded first?

The **second** objective is to help all of us analyze what *usually* drives our bus, so to speak, in our Christian life. (Of course there are many other motivators, but let's think about these for now.) Ask yourself, "Even though I know Grace, am I driven more by fear of failure than I am by the search for success? What does this say about my concept of God?"

The **third** objective is to embrace Grace as a way of life, making fear of failure a thing of the past. (Not that we want to fail on purpose.) I think you know what this means.

b) Fear is big! What does the Bible say?

In Hebrews 2:14 and 15 we see that fear of death enslaves us; Satan uses fear to enslave/control. Do you think we might include other fears here as well, fears of anything and everything, if those fears enslave us, if they control our decisions, actions and feelings? Do you think that to be driven by fear of failure in *legalism* is slavery? Does Satan beat up on you, possibly even control you, with this?

Has it been your experience that, even though such fear is not God's ideal or ultimate motive force in the Kingdom of God (love is), nevertheless the Lord has used our own human primal fear to bring many of us to the Gospel? Praise God! So that ultimately, as the powerful song "Amazing Grace" testifies, "It was Grace that taught my heart to fear, and Grace my fears relieved." You see how consequences (in this case fear) are ultimately part of God's goodness and mercy?

In Genesis 3:10 we see that fear suddenly erupted in Adam and Eve. Apparently fear entered man immediately with sin. What was man most afraid of in Genesis 3? Nakedness? God Himself? Personal responsibility? Anything else? Doesn't it follow that cleansing from sin should deal with fear?

Read I John 4:17–19 and note that fear involves punishment (NASB) and torment (KJV). Is it clear to you how the Lord casts out fear through a process of replacement? Remember what has been said concerning the consequences of unforgiveness: Torment is typical. Fear is a big part of that. Our God has something good to replace every fear.

What else does the Lord use to cast out, to supplant fear? In verse 16 you see faith. Faith in His love! You also see the word "abide." There are three essential "abiding" words: Faith, hope and love, these three abide (I Corinthians 13:13).

Read II Timothy 1:7. Discuss replacement of the spirit of fear (KJV), timidity (NASB). I submit that freedom from fear is the very heart of Godly character. The Holy Spirit is power (with the Gospel, I Corinthians 1:18), love (which casts out fear), and discipline (a sound mind, KJV). Doesn't this Godly character also describe a healthy person? It is ABP grace as opposed to PBA legalism. Do you see how we got there?

c) What type(s) of fear (if any) could be considered God-given assets?

3) It seems that, if we are in Christ, if we have put on the Lord Jesus Christ (Romans 13:14), then we have put on garments that won't make us sweat. I hope the connection between the curse and sweat and the weeds and the cares and worries of this life was clear to you. Now think about this, in Ezekiel 34 it is clear that the priests were not to wear garments that might make them sweat in their ministry to the Lord. That's an interesting concept. It in no way implies that we are to avoid hard work in our service of the Lord. So, do you think it relates to legalism vs. Grace in our service/worship/walk? (It's all worship really.)

4) Have you seen the Lord in His Body, the Church?

a) Does this beauty appear only in your denomination (or non-denomination)? Or is it equally clear in the diversity that cuts across many fellowships, organizations, non-denominations, and denominations?

b) What constitutes this beauty? Do the clay pots help or hinder? Do you think we are good eternal examples of God's Amazing Grace? (Ephesians 2:7)

c) Where is it best to stand in order to see this beauty; outside or inside?

5) What did you learn from the size of your Bible?

a) Does this new perspective effect your action? How?

b) How important is time alone with God? In Chapter 20 in *Grace plus Nothing* I asked you for five and five. Actually, the thought of putting God on the clock (so to speak) is very offensive to me. Having said that, some of you simply needed a reasonable place to begin. Many of you do more than five and five, that's good. Without any condemnation or spiritual pride, how are you doing? Is this strengthening your walk with God?

c) Are you one of those who never gets very far reading the Bible simply because of your desire to understand everything in the Bible the first time you read it? Has this become a paralysis of analysis to you? Has it bogged you down? Maybe not. If it has, can you push yourself to just read?

6) Okay, so where exactly *is* God?

a) God's full and complete presence everywhere, at every point, is referred to by Christian theologians as God's omnipresence and/or immanence. What is the difference between these Biblical concepts and Pantheism?

Pantheism: pan means *all*; and Theos means *God*, i.e., *all God*. Thus, Pantheism believes that the rocks and trees and water, all of the physical realm, the things themselves, are all modes or projections of God.

Do you see the difference? Omnipresence and immanence, as we employ these truths in our Christian faith, mean that God is everywhere, sustaining everything, *but* He is not the things themselves. He is there, in everything, sustaining everything, but it is not *all God*.

b) How do you reconcile God's presence everywhere with the clear Biblical *personhood* of the Father, the Son, and the Holy Spirit? How are these three *distinct* Persons perfectly, absolutely One? No need to apologize if you don't feel adequate to explain Him. Let's just smile and be grateful that we know Him. Still, Scripture supports all of the above. Do you understand that we can easily demonstrate the *fact* of the Godhead in the Bible even though we can't fully explain Him or even wrap our brain around how that's possible?

Do you understand that in Jesus all things hold together and that without Him nothing was made that has been made? Where are these claims in the Bible?

c) Previously we've observed that fear is big, and that's true **if** fear controls us. Otherwise, fear is nothing. **GOD IS BIG**! He is everywhere, at every point in the universe with His whole Person, and we can't even wrap our brains around that. Still, something is radically, totally unique about His presence in and with each believer. What is it? The Bible says, "Christ in you, the hope of glory." (Colossians 1:27) Given that you are no mere Pantheistic mode or projection of God, what is unique about Christ in you?

d) Does Proverbs 21:30 make you smile? Does it make you brave? So, "If God is for us, who is against us?"

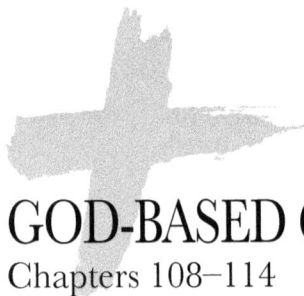

GOD-BASED CHARACTER
Chapters 108–114

Before you begin this discussion:

Review and understand WHAT THE BIBLE SAYS. Volunteers read: Hebrews 10:14 – 18; Psalm 130:4; Proverbs 24:15 and 16; II Corinthians 12:9; 4:5; I John 1:7 – 2:2; Romans 1:16; Acts 4:12; Colossians 1:27.

Discussion Questions:

1) God-Based Character. This book is really about Grace and Godly character. The guiding thesis of *Grace plus Nothing* is that Godly character grows upon the foundation of Grace Alone; both justification and sanctification. We have already mentioned several important aspects of Godly character. Let's think further about character which has grown and matured in Christ. Godly character is more than being a good person. For example, character determines:

How a person responds to failure, to setbacks, and to disappointments.

Quitting vs. Enduring: See Colossians 1:11 and note that this verse mentions not only endurance but endurance with joy.

Teachable vs. Pride. In fact, "teachable" is a very good definition of "humility."

Pursuit of Excellence vs. Perfectionism.

Trusting God vs. Manipulating God.

Dependence upon the Holy Spirit rather than mere human agency and ability.

The attitude that knows, "God doesn't owe me anything!"

No more blaming; we own our issues; we no longer live in denial and rationalization. We are fearless calling our own sin, sin.

Okay, that's just a short list. What would you like to add?

a) When we speak of growing in Godly character and bearing the fruit of the Spirit, upon the foundation of Grace alone, we are talking about the character of Christ developing in us. We are becoming conformed to Him. Read Romans 8:28 and 29 in light of this understanding.

b) Where are *you* in Christ, in the fruit of the Spirit? Does being in Christ mean that you somehow disappear and, therefore, nobody ever sees you anymore, but they only see Jesus? Does Jesus desire such a total obliteration of your personhood?

2) Did you understand why giving up or quitting because of discouragement over our own performance is not a viable option under Grace? Why does the just person (or we could correctly say, the justified person) get up as many times as he/she falls?

Does that describe *character* to you?

3) Do you believe that Jesus staked His life on you? Have you ever thought of that before? Does Colossians 1:27 help open your heart to this reality? Do you think it is correct to say that Jesus believes in you?

Let's discuss this: It is an important aspect of character and dignity that someone else can believe in you. Can Jesus? Under Grace, not only is it possible for you to answer yes to this question, it is inevitable!

Can you think of examples where Jesus demonstrated faith in His disciples/apostles?

4) Why did Jesus preach perfection? Why did He raise the bar so impossibly high? Was He nothing more than a perfectionist?

Can we legitimately and authentically live and model perfection? Does it make any sense at all to preach perfection rather than redemption? Why not just moralize, apart from the Gospel?

5) Effective coaches frequently work on the fundamentals with professional ball players. Is this also a good idea in the Body of Christ?

Are fundamentals and "Fundamentalists" necessarily one and the same thing? I wish with all my heart that the answer to this question could be yes. Don't you?

6) Why do so many believers seem to apply half-measures against sin? Is sin serious enough to die for? Do you take it that seriously? What is God's only cure? I don't apologize one bit for reminding you again. It's fundamental!

7) This also is fundamental: Any teaching that, in effect, raises **anything** to the same level of importance as the finished work of the Cross *for right standing before God* is error. Period! There are many important teachings and practices and attitudes which the Body of Christ needs, but **not one** eclipses Calvary *for right standing before God.*

Therefore, prepare your minds for action, keep sober in spirit, fix your hope completely on the grace to be brought to you at the revelation of Jesus Christ.
I Peter 1:13 NASB

8) Here is the very last verse in the Bible:

The grace of our Lord Jesus Christ be with you all. Amen.
Revelation 22:21 KJV

Note:

1. I have understood the relationship between unforgiveness and torment (in great detail) since about 1969. However, my understanding of the specific concept of boundaries and of the relationship between forgiveness and boundaries derives extensively from Dr. Henry Cloud and Dr. John Townsend in their fine book, *Boundaries, When to Say Yes, When to Say No, To Take Control of Your Life* (Grand Rapids, Michigan 49530: Zondervan, 1992). To the best of my knowledge there are no exact quotes in what I've written concerning the relationship between boundaries and forgiveness, yet my statements on that subject generally follow and/or derive from Cloud's and Townsend's incisive explanation. What I was trying to do was to capsulate the whole thing down to an effective, brief summary. I hope I succeeded. If this section concerning boundaries has spoken to your needs, I strongly suggest that you read Cloud and Townsend: This is far and away the best book I've found on the subject.

Also, just so you know, any similarities between their understanding of forgiveness and mine must be coincidental, based in what the Bible teaches. I've been applying and teaching the exact wording and concepts in my confession and definition of forgiveness, which is in *Grace plus Nothing*, since the early 1970's, always crediting Derek Prince for teaching it to me. None of that came from C and T.

Would to God that more Christian authors and teachers had as firm a grasp on forgiveness as Doctors Cloud and Townsend, including exactly the same definitions and terminology as we are using.

FEEDBACK TO JEFF: Please let me know how this Study and Group Discussion Guide worked for you and for your group so that I can make this tool as effective as is humanly possible. (Please don't send in questions because I don't have time or capability to answer them all.) I would appreciate positive feedback and encouragement as well as negative. Thanks very much. Email appliedgracepubl@aol.com.

PLEASE NOTE: **No books can be ordered at this address.**

www.ingramcontent.com/pod-product-compliance
Lightning Source LLC
LaVergne TN
LVHW081322060426
835509LV00015B/1632